Planning Memorial Celebrations

Planning Memorial Celebrations

A SOURCEBOOK

Rob Baker

Bell Tower
New York

Grateful acknowledgment is made to the following for permission to reprint copyrighted material: Wendell Berry for Stanza I from "Testament," from *The Country of Marriage,* © 1973 by Wendell Berry, used by permission of the author; Catherine A. Falk for selections from "Hmong Funeral in Australia in 1992," Internet article, © 1994 Catherine Falk, used by permission of the author; the Funeral Consumer Information Society of Connecticut, Inc. for material by Josephine Black Pesaresi printed in FCISC Newsletter, Winter 1998 (Vol. 1, No. 1); Alfred A. Knopf for selection from *Tao Te Ching* by Lao Tsu, translated by Gia-fu Feng and Jane English, copyright © 1972 by Gia-fu Feng and Jane English, reprinted by permission of Alfred A. Knopf Inc.; "The Phoenix," from *Old English Poetry,* edited and translated by Charles Kennedy, translation copyright © 1961 by Oxford University Press, Inc., used by permission of Oxford University Press, Inc.; University of Chicago Press for selection from *Young Men and Fire* by Norman Maclean, © 1992 by University of Chicago Press; John Bierhorst for selection from "The Night Chant," translated by Washington Matthews in *Four Masterworks of American Indian Literature,* edited by John Bierhorst, © 1974 by John Bierhorst, published by University of Arizona Press, Charles E. Tuttle Company for selections from *Japanese Death Poems,* compiled and with an introduction by Yoel Hoffmann, © 1986 by Charles E. Tuttle Co., Inc.; Little, Brown and Co. and Curtis Brown, Ltd. for "The Purist," from *I Wouldn't Have Missed It* by Ogden Nash, copyright © 1935 by Ogden Nash, first appeared in *The Saturday Evening Post,* by permission of Little, Brown and Company and Curtis Brown, Ltd.

Copyright © 1999 by Rob Baker

All rights reserved. No part of this book may be reproduced or transmitted in any form or by any means, electronic or mechanical, including photocopying, recording, or by any information storage and retrieval system, without permission in writing from the publisher.

Published by Bell Tower,
201 East 50th Street, New York, New York 10022.
Member of the Crown Publishing Group.

Random House, Inc.
New York, Toronto, London, Sydney, Auckland
www.randomhouse.com

Bell Tower and colophon are registered trademarks of Random House, Inc.

Printed in the United States of America

Design by Jennifer Ann Daddio

Library of Congress Cataloging-in-Publication Data
Baker, Rob.
Planning memorial celebrations: a sourcebook / Rob Baker.
Includes bibliographical references.
1. Memorial service. I. Title.
BV199.M4B35 1999
265'.85—dc21 99-13085
CIP
ISBN 0-609-80404-9

10 9 8 7 6 5 4 3 2 1

First Edition

For
Doro Dooling,
Helen Luke,
and
my father,
Paul Baker:
In Memoriam

Contents

II. Delayed Memorials

Time and Remembrance

No matter what the circumstances may be, the death of someone you love is always a jolt, a sudden shock. Even if you are taking care of a person who has been sick for a long time, you never really expect the exact moment of death; in spite of months or even years of preparation, you are never completely ready.

Time turns upside down on such occasions; it no longer has any steadiness, any reassurance. An hour may seem endless; a week may fly by in an instant. You are in limbo, where any kind of balance or grounding seems difficult, if not impossible.

You face an emptiness, a void, which seems to be yours alone, which you are convinced no one else, no matter how well-meaning, can really understand.

When I confronted my own greatest loss ten years ago, a woman whose counsel I sought put things into perspective: "You now have a very big hole in your life. How do you intend to fill it?" It took me several years to fully understand her meaning: Nothing could fill that vacuum except the very process of grief itself. No person, no thing or activity could substitute or suffice. The loss, the hole, had to be seen, acknowledged, accepted, *remembered*, again and again.

Yet within this limbo, there are immediate important decisions that must be made, difficult responsibilities that you may never have considered. What do you do with the body? Will there be a burial or a cremation? Who will supervise such arrangements? How will friends and relatives be informed?

When you lose someone you love, you are first of all over-whelmed by the loss itself, by the mere fact of no longer being in companionship with your spouse, your lover, your friend or relative who is gone. This book offers a simple checklist for getting through this initial crisis, as well as dealing with another, less easily definable fear: of beginning to *forget*, to lose touch with, the person you've lost—simply no longer remembering, with the same clarity and vividness, all that you have shared.

It is this second loss—this fear of forgetting—that a memorial cel-ebration can especially address. Such services and acts, both private and public, help you confront your loss and keep alive the memory of those who have died—both on a personal, individual level and in a broader, more general way.

This book suggests various methods for nurturing such remem-bering. There are no exact formulas or prescriptions; each remem-brance begins and grows in your own heart, at its own speed. Help can come from many sources: looking at old photographs, listening to music, reading poetry or scripture, being alone in nature, per-forming a ritual ceremony or celebration with others who also remember.

Often you may feel drawn to do or make some *thing* in memory of the person: a poem or other type of eulogy, a calligraphic work, painting, or other handcrafted celebration of the person's life. A spe-cial niche may be set aside where photos and mementos are kept, not exactly as a shrine, but not exactly not as one, either. A kind of very private sanctuary.

Remembering the best and deepest aspects of relationship is akin to remembering the best and deepest aspect of yourself—not your ego, but your soul. This self-remembering brings about a powerful, and empowering, acknowledgment of your own mortality—a rigor-ous honesty that triggers a new sense of being or presence, which helps you through the crisis by linking you with what is best or most essential in all people—our shared humanity. This new sense also links you with something higher still, something that various religions have described as remembrance of God: Sufi *dhikr,* or invocation of the Holy Name; Hindu *japa;* Buddhist *mantra;* centering prayer or prayer of the heart in Christianity. So this simple remembering is something very big indeed.

There, at the center of such remembering, the hole becomes whole again, without completely vanishing. Grief replenishes you, bringing a certain peace and fulfillment. Time begins to flow again. You have learned to let go in remembrance, and, mysteriously, nothing has been truly lost.

. . . Love is not changed by Death,
And nothing is lost and all in the end is harvest.

—EDITH SITWELL, "EURYDICE"

Death is not a period that ends the great sentence of life,
but a comma that punctuates it to more lofty significance.

—DR. MARTIN LUTHER KING

1

First Steps

Someone you love has died. You've confronted deaths before—a friend or relative, perhaps even a parent. But not like this. Never this close. The loss seems unreal, impossible.

You realize you have no idea what to do, where to turn. You need comfort, help, and counseling all at once, but you're not sure whom you should ask or even what the right questions are.

Here is a simple list of what needs to be done. You can use it to help make your own list.

1. Call a doctor or local authority to confirm the death and issue a death certificate. (In cases of sudden or accidental death, emergency medical personnel or the police must also be called. Usually telephoning 911 will bring the appropriate authorities.)
2. Call immediate relatives who may want to see the body before it is removed.
3. Call a religious leader (priest, minister, rabbi, imam) to perform formal prayers or last rites.
4. Decide how the body is to be disposed of: burial, cremation, or donation to medical research.
5. Decide whether the body will remain at home for viewing or be taken to a funeral home or crematorium.

6. Arrange for a permit to move the body to a burial plot or crematorium if a funeral director is not involved.

7. Call those friends and relatives to whom you want to speak personally about the death.

Traditionally, death was a family and a community affair. Preparation of the body for burial, ceremonial viewings, building a coffin, and breaking the ground for a grave were all arranged by the immediate or extended family or by the religious or ethnic group to which the deceased belonged.

In today's modern urban setting, such practices are seldom an option, though a few groups still bury their own.

Chances are, you'll be on your own, which means you'll have to seek the help of professionals—morticians or funeral directors—to coordinate removal of the body from the home or hospital, preparation of the body for viewing or cremation, and carrying out the actual funeral service and burial or cremation procedure; the only alternative is to make all such arrangements yourself.

The advantage of seeking professional help is obvious: Funeral directors take care of all the details—death certificates, permits to move the body, preparation of the body for viewing (sometimes including embalming and cosmetic repair), and burial or cremation.

The disadvantages are that such professionals are costly, and the very services they provide deprive the family or caretakers of what was once a deeply moving personal or communal experience: washing the body, clothing it, holding a wake, building a simple wood coffin, and burial in a family plot or on private land.

Such traditional ways of caring for the dead are still possible, as described in chapters 4, 6, and 7. But these options necessitate careful planning and consultation with local government authorities. All states require death certificates and permits for moving and burying a body. In most cases, burial plots cannot be on private land within city limits or in rural settings of less than a certain acreage.

You need to know all these options exist.

• • •

The first hours and days after a death require a balance between activity and reflection. You find yourself caught between the exhausting prospect of taking charge of the situation too abruptly or completely withdrawing from it into a private realm of numbness and depression. You need to steer a middle course between the two extremes.

The question of whether the body should be on public display—and how, and for how long—must be addressed right away. Various cultures dispose of the body in distinctly different ways (as described in chapter 7) and according to very different time frames. In the Far East, as well as in many Native American tribes, there is a belief that there should be a three-day waiting period to allow the soul to detach itself from the physical body. Jews and Muslims, on the other hand, consider it a great disrespect to the dead not to bury the body as soon as possible, usually before the next sunset following the death. (The orthodox among these religions often forbid embalming and cremation.)

Almost all societies consign the body to one of the four elements: earth (burial), fire (cremation), water (burial at sea), or air (the platform or "sky burials" of Southeast Asia). Occasionally, all four elements are combined, as in the Tibetan and Native American rituals where the corpse is left aboveground, exposed to sun and rain and birds and wild animals for a short period of time, with the final remains being buried in the earth.

Once arrangements for the disposal of the body have been resolved, you can turn next to informing the living: Who needs to be told, how quickly, and by whom? Can some of those you call be delegated to pass the word on to others? When a friend says, "Please let me know if there's anything I can do," he or she usually means it. You should avail yourself of such resources, no matter how strongly you may wish to bear the burden alone. It is not for you to estimate anyone else's share of grief; you have a right to only your portion of it, not to make it an exclusive domain.

Once the important calls have been made, your next obligation is to begin to plan either a funeral or a memorial service. The basic difference between the two is that a funeral service is held when the body is still present; a memorial service takes place when the body has already been buried or cremated. Most funerals, therefore, take place within one to seven days after death; memorial services can be at any time and are usually held a month or so after the burial or cremation. Memorial celebrations thus have the advantage of allowing more time for planning and for the grieving process to be already well under way.

Sometimes more than one memorial service is held: one public, one private; one for one group of friends, another for another group; one in one location, another in a different setting. There are no strict guidelines.

The initial decision of what type of service to hold needs to be made quickly, for a funeral may be only hours or days away, depending on tradition and circumstances. Sometimes the person who died may have left instructions as to her or his preferences in this regard: what should be done, when and where, how elaborate or simple the ceremony should be, who should be invited. If no such wishes were expressed, you must decide what to do.

Seldom should you make this decision alone. Family members, lovers, friends, coworkers, and especially clergy or spiritual advisers can offer valuable support and suggestions. When you open yourself to such help, you let go of much of the burden you have unconsciously become engulfed in or overwhelmed by while strenuously insisting that you can somehow make everything all right on your own.

That letting go leads naturally to a greater letting go in the private realm, when you find yourself truly on your own, with your memories. You can repress those recollections, chase them away like demons, or you can welcome them and embrace them. Each memory of the person can direct you, through honest and open heartache, back into life, where what is now remembered once flourished and existed.

Everything, of course, will still remind you of the person you've lost: songs on the radio, food on the table, objects in a room, places along the road. You can't escape the reminders. You should, in fact, seek them out, be they letters, voices, songs, or other fragments of a past that has not "died" with the departure of someone you loved, but can and will live on, in you, as long as you allow it to do so.

You will also, inevitably, think of your own death: that certainty will both humble you and strengthen you. The admission not only links you to the person you have lost but helps you appreciate more fully the pulse of everyday life around you. This recognition and admission that you, too, are going to die need not be frightening or depressing. By putting a name to death—your own and that of the person you've just lost—you bear up under the threat, rob it of much of its power.

Writer and psychological counselor Helen M. Luke has explored this territory powerfully in an essay entitled "Suffering." She begins with a simple definition of the title word itself.

The Latin verb *ferre* means "to bear," "to carry," and "suffer" derives from it, with the prefix "sub" meaning "under." This is reminiscent of the term "undercarriage"—that which bears the weight of a vehicle above the wheels which is an apt meaning of suffering in human life. . . .

There are, then, two kinds of experiences which we call suffering—that which is totally unproductive, the neurotic state of meaningless depression, and that which is the essential condition of every step on the way to what C. G. Jung has called individuation. Perhaps these images of weight under which we fall and lie in self-pity, or of weight which we carry in full consciousness, may be a guideline in moments of darkness. . . .

Thus, we begin to build the "undercarriage" of suffering upon which the superstructure of our lives may securely rest and under which the wheels may move freely over the earth. The four-wheeled chariot is an ancient symbol of the Incarnation, and the thought of suffering as the undercarriage fits perfectly into this image. Suffering is that which carries the weight of the vehicle, distributing it over the fourfold wheels so that the driver may stand in safety and move towards his chosen goal.[1]

So, as the first day draws to a close, you arrive at another checklist of seven things to do:

1. Begin to plan the funeral or memorial celebration for the person who has died.
2. Involve others close to the deceased in the planning.
3. Build the service around the life and interests of the person being remembered.
4. Welcome the memories of the person who has gone, even when they are painful and make you think of your own mortality.
5. Let go of trying so desperately to hold on to the person who has died.
6. Let go of self-pity and negative resistance.
7. Carry on.

ONE

Memorials at the Time of Death

2

The Standard Solution:
Using the Services
of Professionals

If you have decided on an immediate funeral rather than a delayed memorial service, time is crucial during the next few days. You're going to need help, and you're going to need some rest.

During the day on which the death occurred, you should try to find a few hours to be by yourself, to relax, and, if possible, to get some sleep. If the death was in the afternoon or evening, you may try to keep active until your usual bedtime, but you should not push yourself if exhaustion sets in. If the death was during the night or early morning hours, a long nap during the middle of the day might be advisable. In either case, you'll probably wake up a bit dazed and confused—wondering for a moment if all this is really happening—but in the long run the sleep should clear your mind and give you the strength to continue organizing during the difficult days to come.

This would be a good time to look at your appointment book and cancel all business and personal commitments for the next few days. Though time may seem to have stopped for you, life will continue helter-skelter in the outside world: Your chiropractor or your children's dentist won't necessarily know why you didn't show up for a scheduled visit.

Here is an area where those friends who call and say, "Is there anything I can do to help?" can be of real assistance. Give them a list of calls that need to be made, especially those that you don't have to take care of personally. Let your friends come over and answer the telephone or the doorbell.

As your friends, neighbors, and relatives hear of the death, they will start to telephone or show up at your door with casseroles, rhubarb pies, and roast chickens. A close friend can politely receive these people and relay their gestures of condolence, sorting out the folks you really wish to see or respond to personally. Someone can shop for groceries or cook or clean. Someone else can pick up the dry cleaning, do the laundry, arrange child care.

A few more concerns: Now would be a good time to look for any instructions that the deceased may have left for funeral arrangements. These might be in a family Bible, in a fireproof box in the home, in a personal filing cabinet, or on a home computer. (Important documents relating to the death of a person should not be kept in a bank safe-deposit box unless another member of the family has access to that box, because a death certificate is usually required by the bank before access is allowed.)

Now would also be the appropriate time to collect information needed for the death certificate (such details as mother's maiden name and the deceased's Social Security number may take a bit of research) and for newspaper obituaries, even if these are to be handled by the funeral home. A list of next of kin, colleges or other schools attended, military service records, and job history should be compiled. And because copies of the death certificate are most conveniently ordered at the time the original is filed, it's not too early to determine how many such documents will be needed: for insurance companies, Social Security, taxes and probate; a call to the family lawyer might be necessary.

Perhaps someone else can handle these details, but often you may wish to take care of them yourself, leaving busywork to others.

· · ·

Then back to basics: The first priority will be to complete or continue arrangements for the final disposition of the body. You have probably already made your choice among those options available: standard funeral in a mortuary or church, cremation, home burial, or donation of the body for medical purposes. Whichever you choose, there are forms to be filled out, procedures to be followed, red tape. Here, too, personal friends, colleagues from the office, or fellow church parishioners can be a big help.

If you are of the Baby Boomer generation or slightly older, you may have a distinctly negative attitude toward funeral homes drawn from memories of Liberace selling coffins in the movie *The Loved One* or the tart wit of Jessica Mitford's lambasting the U.S. funeral industry in *The American Way of Death*. But the funeral home option is still the one most people choose by default, especially when no plans have been made by the deceased or the caretakers before death. The reason is simple: one-stop shopping. It's easier to let a professional make all, or at least most, of the arrangements, including casket selection, death certificate, permits for transport and burial, washing and preparation of the body for viewing, provision of a place for visitation as well as a funeral service of some sort, even arrangements for the cemetery.

This convenience comes at a price, of course—and often a hefty one. Funeral directors themselves will insist, as one did on a popular TV talk show during the summer of 1996, that even a low-end funeral now costs about $5,000. No one challenged the figure on the program, but watchdogs of the industry point out that those costs are inflated by at least 200 to 300 percent and that careful consumers who choose a traditional funeral can cut costs dramatically by being alert and taking charge of many of the arrangements themselves.

How do you know if you're getting a fair deal? In years past, grieving families often turned to their priests, rabbis, or pastors for advice. But a growing number of these spiritual advisers have aligned themselves unofficially with a particular mortuary or chain of funeral homes. The old "I'll scratch your back if you scratch mine" approach may be good business, but not for the family of the deceased.

Though this is not true of all clergy—some indeed are among the most vocal advocates of funeral consumer reform—the situation has led to a secular solution to the caveat emptor dilemma in the death industry: the formation of nonprofit memorial societies across the United States and Canada. These independent cooperatives, which grew out of the Grange movement among Midwest farm families in the early 1900s and are now located in almost every state, are resources for advice and assistance to individuals and families confronting all aspects of caring for the dead, especially in regard to funeral homes and governmental red tape. Most of the groups belong to a national coordinating organization called FAMSA (the Funeral and Memorial Societies of America), which has a toll-free number (1-800-765-0107) and a Web site that is chock-full of helpful information and advice:

www.funerals.org/famsa

The executive director of FAMSA is Lisa Carlson, author of *Caring for Your Own Dead*. Self-published in 1987, the book quickly became the standard resource for the funeral-home-alternative movement. It grew out of Carlson's own struggle with Vermont authorities and morticians after her husband's suicide in 1981, when she chose to take control of his cremation. Turning personal tragedy into a lifetime commitment of challenging a system she believes is out of control, Carlson expanded the scope of the original book to *Caring for the Dead: Your Final Act of Love*, published in 1998 and focusing not just on home burial and cremation, as in the earlier volume, but also on working with funeral homes to get fair prices for necessary, minimal services.

Another leading industry watchdog is Father Henry Wasielieski, a Roman Catholic priest in Phoenix who is the driving force behind The Interfaith Funeral Information Committee (IFIC). Its Web site is

www.xroads.com

The site, which contains seventeen documents of information helpful to funeral consumers, covers a wide range of what it calls "rip-offs" in four major areas:

1. Variation in the cost of caskets and funeral services
2. Unnecessary frills added by funeral homes

3. Dangers and inadequacies of "protective seal" caskets
4. Inadvisability of "preplan" funeral policies or arrangements

Citing a 1996 survey by a Houston television station, Father Wasielieski points out prices quoted by funeral homes in the area for the same "lowest-priced traditional funeral and lowest-priced casket." They ranged from $1,495 to $9,910 "for no apparent reason except to obtain up to $8,400 extra profit." The lowest-priced metal casket ranged from $485 to $5,895, direct cremation from $450 to $3,985.

Father Wasielieski (making extensive and dramatic use of colored, boldface, and all-caps type on the Web site, though they've been standardized in the following quotes) advocates a return of funerals to churches, synagogues, and other religious institutions, citing a growing tide of concern "that families and churches need to retake control of their funerals away from morticians and chains—that families need to 'arrange' funerals with their clergy and not with morticians [and] not use morticians' costly, unneeded facilities and assistance; and call upon morticians for only a few things that families might want morticians for (perhaps embalming and some paperwork)." This would restore "the important place of the family church in families' ceremonies, and traditional rites and customs of families and communities—much of which is being distorted by the funeral industry's desires for profit, control and status."[1]

Both IFIC and FAMSA caution against funeral home, cemetery, and insurance company "prepaid packages," suggesting that individuals set up special protected accounts (called Totten Trusts; see page 53) at their own banks instead. The two groups are also particularly concerned with the trend toward large national and even international funeral chains: The largest, Service Corporation International (SCI), located in Houston, owned a mind-boggling 2,795 mortuaries, 325 cemeteries, and 138 crematoria as of March 1996. Such a megacorporate trend not only compromises personal local service, the two groups feel, but raises serious questions about a death industry monopoly by four or five major players.

* * *

Thanks to the type of pressure exerted by FAMSA and IFIC, the Federal Trade Commission (FTC) issued its Funeral Industry Practices Rule in 1984 and its Revised Rule in 1994. The major sections deal with forcing funeral homes to give written price disclosures and outlawing various "misrepresentations" by the industry. Among its stipulations are the following:

1. Funeral homes must disclose pricing by telephone or in writing to anyone asking about their services, including the retail prices of "all caskets and alternative containers" as well as those of the "outer burial containers" (the burial vaults, grave boxes, and grave liners now demanded by many cemeteries to "prevent earth settling" on top of a casket).

2. They must also offer, in writing, a general price list of optional services, including the following itemized costs:

   • Forwarding remains to another funeral home
   • Receiving remains from another funeral home
   • Direct cremation (with or without provision of alternative container)
   • Immediate burial (no funeral service)
   • Transfer of body from place to death to funeral home
   • Embalming services
   • Other "preparation of the body" (washing, dressing, cosmetics, hairstyling, etc.)
   • Use of facilities and staff for viewing and visitation
   • Use of facilities and staff for funeral ceremony
   • Use of facilities and staff for memorial service
   • Use of equipment and staff for graveside service
   • Hearse
   • Limousine(s)
   • Cash advance items (honorariums to clergy, musicians, etc.)

3. Service providers specifically can *not* tell customers that state or local law requires that a deceased person be embalmed

"when such is not the case"; state that embalming is required for cremation, direct immediate burial, or a closed casket funeral with no viewing or visitation (when refrigeration is available and when state or local law does not require embalming after a certain period of time); allege that state or local laws or regulations, or particular cemeteries, require outer burial containers unless that is truly the case; pretend that funeral goods or funeral services will delay the natural decomposition of human remains for a long or indefinite time or will "protect the body from gravesite substances"; or mark up "cash advance items" (honorariums and other purchases) on the price list so the sum stated appears to be what is paid to the subcontractee and does not reflect the markup.

4. The rule also states that the service provider cannot deny customers one good or service simply because they don't use another service, or charge any extra processing fees not allowed by law.

Contained at the top of the above-mentioned written price list must be the following statement: "The goods and services shown below are those we can provide to our customers. You may choose only the items you desire. If legal or other requirements mean you must buy any items you did not specifically ask for, we will explain the reason in writing on the statement we provide describing the funeral goods and services you selected."

In other words, funeral homes cannot deny specific services—some of which they alone are allowed to provide by various state laws, such as issuing transport permits—just because a customer does not want to buy their whole package. (They can still, however, charge outrageously high fees for issuing those permits and non-negotiable "service fees," and many of them still do.) Thus by law, customers are allowed to supply their own caskets (or even build their own) and reject such supplied services as embalming, outer burial containers (unless required by the cemetery), in-house viewings, and even transport to the cemetery in the company hearse—as long as they abide by the relatively few required regulations set up by state and local authorities. A listing of these specific regulations can be obtained from FAMSA (either a local group or the national office; see Memorial Societies in the United States, page 139 or from local authorities, usually without having to request them from the funeral homes directly.

Here is a standard list of questions that you need to consider, even if you choose a fairly traditional cemetery burial and services of some sort (or even none at all) under the overall auspices of a funeral director:

1. Whether or not to embalm the body
2. Whether or not to prepare and enhance the body for public viewing
3. What type of casket to select
4. Whether or not an outer burial container is desirable or needed
5. Whether to hold a funeral service and, if so, where
6. How to transport the body from the funeral home or other funeral site to the cemetery or other grave site
7. Whether or not to hold a graveside service

All of these choices will obviously affect the cost of the funeral package. And you should watch especially for the cost of such added services as the following:

1. Funeral director processing and filing the death certificate
2. Funeral director placing the obituary
3. Funeral director arranging for (prepaying honorariums to) clergyman and musicians for a service
4. Funeral director providing guest book and thank-you cards
5. Funeral director arranging pallbearers or ushers for the service

All of these can be arranged almost as easily by your friends or yourself—unless you feel that paying the professional is worth the price.

Most controversial of all the above-cited issues are embalming, presentation of the corpse for public viewing, and casket pricing and construction.

In spite of the fact that embalming is virtually unknown outside the United States and has been deemed by the Centers for Disease Control to be ineffective at stemming the spread of communicable diseases (one of its alleged primary purposes), morticians in the United States continue to drain the blood and body fluids out of corpses and replace them with preservatives—though at least they cannot now do so legally without the family's consent. Even this idea of preserving the body—the other primary purpose of the process—is highly suspect. The chemicals delay the decomposition process by only a few days (if that long), and they are not nearly as effective as refrigeration or air-conditioning, which are less expensive as well as less invasive.

Nonetheless, morticians tend to sing the praises of embalming. No less a source than *The New Grolier Multimedia Encyclopedia* (1993 edition) maintains that embalming "consists of chemically disinfecting and temporarily preserving the dead human body"—neither of which it actually does. The entry continues: "The primary objectives are to remove the body fluids, to replace them with disinfecting chemicals that reduce the growth of micro-organisms, and to introduce preserving chemicals that delay the decomposition of cellular structures . . . to reduce as much as possible the danger of infection or contagion to the public."[2] This highly scientific explication refers to a very unscientific procedure dreamed up by mid-nineteenth-century morticians in France and Italy, aping a vastly different process (for a vastly different purpose) in ancient Egypt. (Hawaii recognizes that embalming actually enhances the spread of communicable diseases rather than reducing it and prohibits it in such cases.)

Somewhat related to this attempt at postponing the inner decomposition of the body is the attention paid to the outside of the corpse.

Though traditional societies and religious cultures have almost always cleaned, prepared, and dressed their dead for their funerary journey—usually in a simple white cloth or shroud, perhaps anointed with oils or perfumes—never in history has so much attention been paid to superficialities of cosmetic enhancement and costuming as is done by morticians in the United States. Frequently, corpses bear little if any resemblance to the person the mourners knew a day, a week, or a month earlier, especially if the person was ill and suffering. Instead the corpses are reduced to a flat sameness of facial features and expression, often made to look much younger or much more proper than they were in life. ("A man does not have to be dressed in a business suit and tie when he is placed in a casket for viewing," writes D. Allen Polen in *The Funeral Arrangement Choice Guide.* "Dress him as he lived."[3] Suits for the businessmen; flannel shirts and blue jeans for a lumberjack, a woodworker, a harvester.)

It's up to you to determine whether such a public viewing is necessary at all—beyond the need of the family to see the person one last time, in private, before the funeral (in which case only the basic amenities need to be prepared). If such a choice is made, you should determine how you want the corpse to be represented: as the person was in life or as some mortician's concept of bland propriety. Which counts more, the public self or the private persona? Is the wig properly placed (the way he or she actually wore it), the eyeglasses, the false teeth? If you are not comfortable with the look presented—or that any look should be presented at all—others are likely to share your discomfort.

The next question involves yet another level of exterior, material concern—another layer of superficiality, you might call it—the casket housing the body, and the second casket that in turn houses that: the outer burial container. The first is for presentation, for show—to make the body look comfortable, almost luxurious, for its passage; the second is for protecting her or him from water and dirt and even minute forms of life.

Protecting death from life seems an odd construct: What we're talking about, to use a phrase from the FAMSA Web site, is really just "a box within in a box" (the body within a casket—both within a third box, if the outer container is added).

This is where the canny funeral director has you up against the wall: He or she shows you a plain wood coffin (maybe, but not always), then a cheap metal one, then one of pressed wood lined in silk, then one with a padded and pillowed interior and beautiful gold tubing, and on and on. You want the *best* resting place for your deceased, of course (it is gently suggested). No matter that the calculator just keeps clicking every step you move up the coffin chain.

A casket used to be a plain pine box, made by hand by someone who loved the deceased. A simple box for a simple act: burying the dead, returning dust to dust, with a fragile, natural, intentionally temporary barrier in between.

Then comes the question of "protective seal" caskets, which are supposed to keep water and other "foreign elements" out of the casket once it is underground. The implication is that this type of casket will allow the body to remain just as it looked before the casket lid was closed and that your loved one will simply stay there, in a box within a box within a box, unchanging through eternity.

In truth, nothing can stop the process of natural decomposition that has begun: not the embalming, not the cosmetics and three-piece suit, not the sealed casket, not the outer burial container.

As Father Wasielieski points out (perhaps a bit graphically for some tastes), these futile attempts to beat time can backfire rather horribly:

All morticians know that "Protective Seal" metal caskets are not protective, but destructive—starting severe damage to every body immediately after the casket is closed. . . . They all know that these caskets destroy your relatives' bodies within a month or two—by liquefying the soft parts of the bodies and causing high pressure which rapidly bloats them completely out of shape. In addition, the high pressure in many caskets bursts the seals, blowing the liquefied body parts out of the caskets (especially in mausoleums) . . . sometimes blowing granite fronts off the crypts.[4]

As the FTC Revised Rule tries to make clear, neither the casket (no matter how expensive, no matter how well sealed) nor the outer container in any way preserves the body or protects it from the elements of nature (to which it is destined to return anyway).

A pattern becomes clear: The more the funeral director offers or arranges, the less you do, and the less involved you become, not only with the process but with death (life) itself. Many of the traditions associated with death and mourning of even a hundred years ago have been curtailed or abandoned: the wake, the funeral procession, the church funeral, and (perhaps most important) a period of formal mourning during which the grieving behave—and are treated—differently. Pomp and circumstance have been jettisoned for primping and conventionality. Funerals have become increasingly plain and ordinary at the same time they have become overpriced and antisymbolically "ecumenical." They take place, as Wilfrid Sheed has remarked, not "in church at all, but in synthetic chapels where, in place of a priest, the funeral director administers empathy and semiclassical music."[5]

As funeral historian James Farrell wrote at the end of his study *Inventing the American Way of Death, 1830–1920:*

> The paraphernalia of the American way of death keep people at one remove from their own feelings. . . . This social convention developed historically, but it continues today, as Americans delegate control of death and the funerals to specialized funeral service personnel. Consequently, funerals are custom-made only in the same sense that automobiles are, and the price we pay for paying our last respects in the American way of death is the price of our personality, which we have purposely withheld from the funeral. By our passive role in directing our funerals, we have transformed an important rite of personal passage into an impersonal rite of impassivity.[6]

Not everyone chooses to be impassive, however. When Supreme Court Justice Hugo Black died in 1971, after thirty-five years on the high court, he left specific instructions to his children regarding his funeral: He wanted to keep it simple and cheap, with no open casket.

No problem, under ordinary circumstances: Most children do their best to fulfill the explicit wishes of a parent who has died. But when your father was a Supreme Court justice and his funeral is to be held at the National Cathedral in Washington, D.C., with the president, plus lots of judges and politicians in attendance and a eulogy by the cathedral's bishop, Francis Sayre, it's hard to keep things simple or cheap.

Nonetheless, when three of Justice Black's children and two of his cohorts on the Supreme Court went to select his coffin, they remembered his request. His daughter, Josephine Black Pesaresi, recalls:

The casket room was elegantly appointed. The carpeting, wall paneling and piped in music set a tone for coffin shopping in undisputed good taste. On entering, one's eye was immediately drawn to the extreme left wall where a superbly crafted dark wood coffin, softly spot-lighted to show the fine wood grain, was perched high on a velvet-draped dais. It looked like a throne coffin.

However, we were steered counter clockwise, starting our search at the right. The caskets were arranged head to toe in a semicircle leading up to the throne coffin, and it was obvious that we were going from least to most expensive.

The first coffin we came to—the cheapest—was covered with pink organza, pink satin bows, with a pink ruffled skirt around the bottom. Tasteless and frilly, it seemed totally out of place. The next ones were also cloth-covered, but the cloth looked increasingly more expensive. Our salesman was surprised that we even glanced at these, let alone asked their prices, and indirectly dismissed these as a final resting-place for a man of importance. He began to hurry us on until we came to the throne coffin.

We stood in front of this masterpiece of craftsmanship with heads slightly bowed reverently. "This," the coffin salesman said, "is the worthy resting place for a Justice of the United States Supreme Court." When we asked the cost of the throne coffin, he did not immediately give a dollar amount. He noted that while it was the most expensive, he knew that the price was not our main concern when burying a man of my father's stature. Cost considerations would be unworthy. This response was a big mistake and backfired immediately.

Suddenly, almost simultaneously, we looked at each other, smiling as my father's directive hit us full force—cheap. We moved to another emotional dimension—common at wakes—going from a deep grieving sadness to an almost playful mood. Right there, in that elegant room, we knew that together we could do one last thing for my father. No one was going to talk us out of cheap! When pressed, the coffin salesman allowed that the throne coffin cost thousands of dollars. That settled that.

We dispersed, zigzagging around the room, separately appraising the caskets and asking prices down to the penny. All of the polished wood caskets were soon dismissed as too expensive. It had to be a cloth-covered one. To the salesman's horror, Justice White began to scrutinize the first pink organza coffin and then asked what was under the frills. The salesman said it was just a plain, unfinished pine box. Then someone asked about the most expensive cloth-covered casket. That, too, was a plain pine box. When asked the difference between the boxes, the salesman—now completely befuddled—whispered that the more expensive had a "better shape." We looked and thought the shapes were identical.

Huddling for a final conference, someone asked, "Shall we get the pink, the cheapest?" and we all gave a resounding "YES." We said we would buy the pink for $165 with the cloth stripped off. The salesman said that was impossible, it would look terrible. We, however, wanted to see for ourselves since this was our coffin of choice. First one of us pulled away a little cloth to take a peek, then another ripped more forcefully, and finally we all started ripping off the fabric with careless abandon. Off came the bows, the coffin skirt, and all but a few patches of stubbornly glued pink organza. There stood a perfectly fine plain pine box. The debris littered the elegant carpet, but we were practically euphoric. We had followed my father's directive almost to a tee, with added bonus of deflating pretensions in this very pretentious room (though my father would have felt some compassion for the poor coffin salesman).

When we went into the office to settle the bill, the funeral home director, now understanding our zeal for cheap, asked timidly about filling in the nail holes and sanding down the glue spots. With a closed casket visitation at the funeral home and a display at the cathedral, they felt their reputation was at stake. We agreed, if nothing was added to the bill, and were assured nothing would be.

Dean Sayre of the National Cathedral made a final request in the spirit of my father's wishes. He asked that at the funeral we have the casket displayed without the American flag or flowers on top of it. He, as my father, had long been concerned about the excessive cost of burying the dead and the financial burden this put on living loved ones. He wanted people to see that the cost of a coffin did not symbolize the abiding love of the living for the dead, nor did it reflect the stature of a man.[7]

3

First Alternative:
Cremation

I went behind the scenes at the end of the service and saw the real tiling [of the crematorium]. People are afraid to see it; but it is wonderful. I found there the violet coffin opposite another door, a real unmistakable furnace door. When it lifted there was a plain little chamber of cement and firebrick. No heat. No noise. No roaring draught. No flame. No feel. It looked cool, clean, sunny, though no sun could get there. You would have walked in or put your hand in without misgiving. Then the violet coffin moved again and went in feet first. And behold! The feet burst miraculously into streaming ribbons of garnet coloured lovely flame, smokeless and eager, like pentecostal tongues, and as the whole coffin passed in it sprang into flame all over, and my mother became that beautiful fire.[1]

This description by George Bernard Shaw of his mother's cremation, taken from a letter to a friend, treats the action matter-of-factly, with the sort of open-eyed objectivity we might expect from the great British dramatist and wit. What he depicts is a natural operation, cleanly and neatly executed, with no fiddle-faddle.

Cremation is exactly that, at least in the West. It is a quintessentially secular way to deal with death and is often accompanied by no ritual or ceremony such as those associated with funerals.

Touted as a space-efficient alternative to cemeteries, cremation is now the preferred method of body disposition in England and Japan. In most of the United States, some 17 percent of bodies are cremated; the percentage is higher in California (40 percent) and Florida (35 percent).

The cremation process is much as Shaw described it. A body is placed in a simple casket or "alternative container" (usually plywood, pressed wood, or even heavy cardboard—no plastic or fiberglass), then the container goes into a brick oven, usually powered by gas or electricity, and is heated for about two hours until the body is reduced to bone and the container to ash. These remains (usually referred to by the rather ugly neologism "cremains") are then cooled and pulverized, to make sure that no large bone fragments are left intact (which could cause difficulties if they were scattered on public land or at sea and were later found by or reported to law enforcement officials). The remains are then turned over to the survivors, in either a plain box or a decorative urn, usually the following day.

The remains can be kept by the family (usually in the decorative urn), buried (sometimes in a garden area of a conventional cemetery), scattered over land or sea, or placed in special mausoleum-type structures called columbaria.

Cremation is a popular choice with some because of:

- Price (a third or less than the cost of the cheapest funeral-home services)
- Convenience of arrangements (A permit to cremate is still required as well as a transport permit to the crematorium, but arrangements for viewing, services, and cemetery operations are generally not involved.)
- Mobility of final remains (They can even be sent via Express Mail or FedEx, though UPS still refuses if it knows what's in the package.)
- Romantic appeal of being able to scatter the "ashes" almost anywhere on land (except in California) or sea: on a

mountaintop, in a river, in a favorite park or the garden of
a vacation home—or to keep them in an urn on your
living room mantel

The negative trade-offs for these advantages are directly linked to
the positives: the absence of any funeral service or viewing (except in
rare cases, when a casket is rented and a viewing is held in the crematory chapel prior to cremation) and the impermanence of having
the remains scattered or in a movable container—there is no final resting place, no grave to visit, though one could go to wherever the scat-
tering took place, or visit the urn.

Cremation is the preferred method of disposal for the eight thousand Americans who die abroad each year, and it is also usually the
method used if visiting foreigners or recent immigrants die in the
United States and survivors wish their bodies to be shipped back to
their native country (the high cost of shipping embalmed bodies
being prohibitive in both cases).

Cremation has a history and tradition all its own; it has existed for
thousands of years in Russia, India, and even ancient Babylon. Julius
Caesar was cremated, as were Attila the Hun and Percy Bysshe Shelley, the British poet who drowned while swimming off the coast of
Greece. Shelley's body couldn't be shipped home to England because
of local health conditions in Greece.

The ancient Greeks frequently used cremation (especially for soldiers), as did the Romans and the Vikings. Buddhists and Native
Americans often prefer it. But Muslims and Orthodox Jews consider
it a sacrilege and usually forbid it.

In India, Hindu widows followed their dead husbands onto the
pyre until the practice, known as suttee or sati, was outlawed by the
British early in the nineteenth century (although it persisted in many
rural areas much longer).[2] In Richard Wagner's *Götterdämmerung*,
Brunnhilde celebrates the same tradition, jumping onto Siegfried's
funeral pyre and taking most of heaven and earth with her into cos-
mic destruction.

• • •

Here are a few more details, if you are considering cremation:

- Pacemakers must be removed from the body prior to cremation.
- Jewelry, glasses, and the like should be taken from the body prior to the procedure; the crematorium is not responsible for them.
- Alternative containers for cremation should be no more than 38 inches wide and 30 inches tall.
- If a cardboard container is used, a firm board should be placed under the body before it is transported, especially if the body is large or overweight;
- Authorization to cremate must be obtained, either from the deceased (in writing prior to death) or the next of kin; if survivors are divided over the procedure, the crematory may refuse services.
- Cremation must be done within forty-eight hours in most states; otherwise, the body will have to be embalmed or refrigerated first.

The choice between cremation and burial remains a dilemma for many. As surgeon Richard Selzer has put it:

> The more I think about it, the better I like burial in the ground. People are of two kinds, you know. Those that love nothing more than to be wrapped up snug by their environs, and those who yearn to be unfettered, airborne, wafted. Knowing this, it is not at all amazing that some prefer interment while others opt for cremation. It is not a reasoned choice; it is a matter of temperament.[3]

4

Second Alternative: Private Service and Home Burial

What if you are turned off completely by both funeral homes and the idea of cremation? Is there no way to keep your dead at home, hold a simple ceremony there, then bury the body in the backyard, the way American pioneers did for generations?

It's not quite that easy, even with the aid of the Internet or Lisa Carlson's *Caring for the Dead*. Funeral directors have been lobbying American lawmakers for decades now, and funeral rights activists have a long way to go before they catch up with them in most locations.

In many states (particularly in the West and Southwest), it is still possible to bury a body on private property in rural areas, if you have the proper permits and you (or your tribe or religious group) own the land. Certain restrictions apply regarding distance from water sources and power lines; local zoning rules should be checked.

Other states require that a body be buried in an "established cemetery," though what constitutes such a cemetery is often vague (are abandoned rural church cemeteries included?), as is whether and how new ones might become "established." (One spiritual group in

Indiana managed to establish a new private cemetery when its leader was buried, but only on the condition that the cemetery be on at least twenty-five acres of property owned by the group. They had only twenty-four acres and had to acquire an extra acre from a neighbor before the permit could be issued.)

If you opt for burial in a public cemetery, you can still handle arrangements by yourself. This would include:

1. Buying the plot
2. Hiring a gravedigger to open and close the grave
3. Obtaining a burial permit from the town clerk or board of health (ironically, this sometimes entails going through a local mortician)
4. Purchasing a grave liner (a concrete enclosure for the casket) from the cemetery (or a third party) if one is required by the cemetery

You can keep the body at home and prepare it for burial yourself or with the help of family, neighbors, or members of your religious group. (Orthodox Jews, Muslims, and Gypsies continue to do this regularly.) You can hold your own wake or ceremony, and you can (in many states) transport the body to the burial site. If the body is not already on your own property, law enforcement officials will require a transport permit, which usually stipulates that a funeral director must be at the other end to receive the body and, in some cases, to oversee the burial. (Many funeral directors are the delegated officers who issue transport and burial permits.)

You have the right to buy a coffin from any casket retailer or build one of your own (even if you are using a funeral home's services). Often a relative may have carpentry skills; if not, a plain pine box coffin is relatively easy to construct. (Ernest Morgan has simple instructions for doing so in his book *Dealing Creatively with Death: A Manual of Death Education and Simple Burial*.[1])

If you are handling all the arrangements yourself, you will also have to make sure that the death certificate is properly executed. This involves picking it up from the relevant government agency and mak-

ing sure that it is signed and properly filled out by the attending doctor (if death comes in a hospital) or by the deceased's regular physician or the local coroner (if death comes at home). If death is by
accident or is otherwise unexpected, emergency medical personnel or
the police will have to be contacted. The police and coroner may
require an autopsy if the death is deemed suspicious.

After the doctor or coroner has completed his or her portion of
the death certificate, you will have to fill out the rest of it. This has
to be done very carefully, with a typewriter or black ink. No era-
sures, corrections, or correction fluid are allowed; if you make a mistake, you have to start over. The death certificate requires a great deal
of specific information, including race, nationality, date and state of
birth, marital status, military service history, Social Security number,
occupation, and parents' names (including mother's maiden name)—
all in addition to the information that the doctor or coroner must
supply, which includes "immediate cause of death," "condition
antecedent to the immediate cause," "underlying cause of death," and
"contributory cause of death" (any other important disease or condition that did not directly contribute to the death).

Carlson's *Caring for the Dead* lists state requirements and funeral
laws (as well as information on cremation and bequeathal to medical
schools) for all fifty states and is an invaluable resource for anyone
planning the process alone. Some of the stipulations may seem quaint
or amusing: In Alabama, for example, funeral directors may not hold
a body "for payment"; in Alaska and Iowa, coal mining is not per-
mitted within a hundred feet of a cemetery; in Kentucky, the death
certificate can be signed by a dentist or a chiropractor as well as a
physician; and in Nevada, livestock may not be pastured in a cemetery. Nevertheless, it is essential to be apprised of these regulations if
home burial or other funeral-home-independent acts are undertaken.
Keep in mind especially:

- Death certificate requirements
- Transportation and burial permits
- State or local burial restrictions
- Local zoning laws

So, all in all, a do-it-yourself burial is not easy. The grieving process is interrupted by, if not swamped with, bureaucratic red tape, forms, and permits—roadblocks at every turn by funeral directors who simply may be trying to preserve their own livelihoods. (Carlson estimates that there are two to three times more funeral homes in most states than the death rate can support.)

But the extra effort required for a do-it-yourself burial may be worth it: Standing on a small hill looking down on a private grave in Montana or Indiana, you know just how special the result is from the struggle someone endured to go against the trend and preserve an ancient tradition or to allow someone's strongly felt personal last wishes to be met.

Carlson's second husband, Steve, records the process he went through for his mother. It was a completion, a closure of a life well lived.

My brothers and I transported the casket in my pickup truck and spent the next eight hours digging the grave by hand. It was hard work in clay soil with many large rocks. We were eager to meet all legal requirements, so we dug the grave six feet deep. . . . The task culminated weeks of shared work and shared emotions that brought the four of us closer together than anything else we could have possibly done. For many years we had been separated by distance, careers, and individual commitments. By working together at a time of great need we renewed and strengthened our family bonds. For my brothers and me, the private burial was the best way to say good-bye to our mother.[2]

5

Third Alternative:
Donation of the Body for
Medical Purposes

There is one other solution for final disposition: donating the body as a whole or in part for medical purposes, either as a medical school teaching cadaver or as organ transplants.

In the latter case, the removal of the organ or organs generally must take place immediately after death, so this is usually feasible only when the death occurs in a hospital equipped to execute the procedure.

Many states have an "organ donation" form on the back of an individual's driver's license. This does not guarantee that donation will take place, however. Those wishing to make such donations (of a specific organ or organs, or of "whatever is needed") should also secure Uniform Donor Cards, which should be filled out and carried in their purses or wallets as well. The card is available from FAMSA or from The Living Bank, P.O. Box 6725, Houston, TX 77265; Medic Alert, Turlock, CA 95380; or the National Kidney Foundation, 2 Park Avenue, New York, NY 10016. (Persons with such wishes should also make sure that their families or caregivers know of—and agree to—these wishes as well.)

There is a great need, always, for hearts, kidneys, and livers, as well as eye corneas (The latter sometimes can be removed and preserved if death occurs at home by calling your local eye bank.) The donor of major organs needs to be in good health; heart donors must usually be under thirty-five years of age.

Generally a standard funeral, with or without viewing, can take place after organ donation. Cremation is often an option as well. (In cases of deaths that occur abroad, where the body will normally be cremated rather than embalmed and sent home at great expense for burial, organ donation is especially viable.)

Bodies donated to medical schools for research (sometimes referred to as bequeathals) cannot have experienced major trauma (as in an automobile accident), have been autopsied, or be missing any organs: In other words, the same body can't be both an organ donor and a medical cadaver. The schools also require that the bodies be disease free and in relatively healthy condition—not obese, not too old—and that they not be embalmed by an undertaker. (An embalming procedure totally different from that used for burial is used by the institution to preserve the organs and tissues for up to a year and a half for study.)

Arrangements must usually be made with the medical school prior to death, using a form supplied by the school. In some cases, the schools pay for local transportation of the corpse (though not usually long-distance transport); sometimes the family must pay. No payment is made to the survivors for the gift.

Schools will sometimes allow a short period of viewing of the body in a funeral home prior to picking up the body, as long as the body is not embalmed by the undertaker.

Occasionally, schools reject a body (for the reasons cited above), even if prior arrangements have been stipulated. In such cases the school generally pays for cremation or returns the body to the family for disposal. (The family should thus have an alternate plan in mind.)

The remains of the body are cremated after the study period concludes; the ashes are either scattered in a special garden at the school or returned to the family on request.

•   •   •

The medical donation alternative may be a valid choice for you, especially if ceremonial closure with the body of the deceased is not a priority. It is the quintessential secular humanist response—an act of genuine public-mindedness and generosity. Because of your gift, someone else may see or live or learn about anatomy.

On the other hand, you may be more than a bit uncomfortable with the idea of someone walking around with the organ of someone you were close to, or the thought of that person's form being clinically examined while lying on a cold metal table, day after day, by a group of medical students who see it primarily as an object, not the remains of a specific person.

Such questions need to be seriously addressed and considered before you or the other survivors make a decision. Body donation may be the easiest and cheapest solution to disposition, but like all easy answers it comes at a cost, which in this case may be the peace of mind of the survivors.

Because the issue is so touchy—symbolically, emotionally, spiritually—medical schools almost never accept donations if there is disagreement among the survivors over the procedure. (Hospitals seeking organ transplants are often a good deal less circumspect in trying to persuade the family of someone on life support to make organ donation decisions during this time of great emotional stress.)

If it is possible to ascertain the feelings of the person whose body is going to be involved—either in writing or in conversation before death—this is helpful. Most states will legally uphold those rights.

In some cases, however, the wishes of the survivors may be at odds with what the deceased has stipulated, presenting yet another moral (and sometime legal) dilemma. It is best if the matter can be discussed and resolved in advance.

6

A Brief Background of American Funeral Customs

Until the time of the Civil War, most Americans buried their own dead. Funeral services, wakes, and visitations were held at home, and the body was buried in the churchyard or a family cemetery. There were exceptions, of course, in urban settings, but the standard pretty much held true: Church and family members did everything from washing and dressing the body—often in a specially sewn shroud—to making the coffin and digging the grave. Celebrations of the death of a loved one were personal and religious: Survivors were closely involved with the process of handling, viewing, and saying a personal good-bye to their dead.

The first undertakers usually plied their trade part-time, often working out of furniture stores (a casket after all being a kind of cabinet) or livery stables (horses were needed to draw the hearse). These early businessmen, who did not yet call themselves funeral directors, supplied a service to the community, working closely with local clergymen and the families of the deceased.

Over time, these new professionals added more and more services—and more and more costs. Funerals became big business with the introduction of embalming, cosmetic enhancement, mortuary viewings, solemn processions (by foot or horse and carriage originally, then by automobile), elaborate graveside procedures, not to mention administrative services involving death certificates, transport and burial permits, and handling such details as hiring a minister or an organist for the funeral or placing an obituary in the local paper.

Meanwhile, a separate industry was growing. Cemeteries, which had once been church owned or private family graveyards, became commercial ventures: Their business was to charge not just for the space of a funeral plot but for opening and closing a grave, erecting a monument, and upkeep of the site (providing work for three other categories of workers as well: gravediggers, monument engravers, and groundsmen).

As this business of death—of undertaking, of funeral direction, of mortuary science—grew, the general public's involvement in the process waned. People now attended a funeral the way they did a concert or a high school graduation. They were observing rather than participating. Death became distant, a necessary evil or an interruption of daily routine, not the integral and essential part of life it had been before.

In his classic essay "The Pornography of Death," British social psychologist Geoffrey Gorer noted a similar trend in England, where death suddenly became "pornographic," more unmentionable in polite company than sex. The longtime Anglo-Saxon custom of mourning—during which the family of the dead wore black clothes, veils, and armbands for a varying period of time to honor the dead and set themselves apart from the chaotic "colors" of ordinary life—was abandoned as "old-fashioned," and something very essential was lost. In his introduction to his full-length study, *Death, Grief, and Mourning,* Gorer recalls that, following his brother's death in the early 1960s:

A couple of times I refused invitations to cocktail parties, explaining that I was in mourning; the people who invited me responded to this statement with shocked embarrassment as if I had voiced some appalling obscenity. Indeed, I got the impression that, had I stated that the invitation clashed with some esoteric debauchery I had arranged, I would have had understanding and jocular encouragement; as it was, the people whose invitations I had refused, educated and sophisticated though they were, mumbled and hurried away. They clearly no longer had any guidance from ritual as to the way to treat a self-confessed mourner; and, I suspect, they were frightened lest I give way to grief, and involve them in a distasteful upsurge of emotion.[1]

Consider the alternative, the way Gorer's sister-in-law reacted to her husband's death:

She did not wear black clothes nor ritualize her mourning in any way; she let herself be, almost literally, eaten up with grief, sinking into a deep and long-lasting depression. At the period when she most needed help and comfort from human society she was left alone.[2]

As a social scientist, Gorer had studied the death and mourning customs of many cultures and realized that almost all of them had certain rituals to allow individuals and the community to deal with death. For individuals it involved wearing certain clothes, shaving the head or cutting the hair, and removing themselves from the ordinary trivialities of life for a certain period of time. For the community—which also needed to respond to the death of one of its members in an appropriate way—mourning centered on the ritual ceremony of the funeral itself, a coming together to honor and say good-bye to the dead.

French death historian Philippe Ariès has been equally outspoken about modern trends in the funeral industry, especially those involving the beautification of the corpse. "In order to sell death, it had to be made friendly," he stated in a lecture series on "Western Attitudes Toward Death" at Princeton University in 1974. The following year, he wrote: "The idea of making a dead person appear alive as a way of paying one's last respects may well strike us as puerile and preposterous. . . . But it . . . testifies to a rapid and unerring adaptation to complex and contradictory conditions of sensibility. This is the first time in history that a whole society has honored the dead by pretending they were alive."[3]

Concurrent with all this, cemeteries likewise became more and more sterile and uniform; monuments—deemed as having become too elaborate and personalized—were replaced with ground-level plaques (all the better to mow you with, my dear) and restrictions on planting flowers or shrubs or anything to personalize the space.

Contrast this with cemeteries at the turn of the century or earlier that were planned for variety and beauty. Guarding against overcrowding, their planners added meandering footpaths, lily ponds, large statues, flowers, and landscaping. The public cemetery in Lexington, Kentucky, attracts art students from colleges around the state to come and paint its flowers and ponds, especially the glorious field of tulips that bloom each spring.

In some rural areas, families still care for and bury their own dead. Black Americans, especially in nonurban settings, continue to celebrate the dead with ceremonies full of tradition: good food, good company, "dressing up" in their best and brightest clothes, and lots and lots of music and eulogizing.

In Appalachian eastern Kentucky, two sociologists found a "strong sense of kinship and neighborhood" at funerals; it reflected the care of the elderly and the dying, who were "comforted, attended to, and remained an active part of the social matrix until death."[4] (No nursing homes and old folks centers here, and death occurred at home, surrounded by one's family, not in a hospital.)

Sometimes in these rural communities, burials would take place at the time of death, but the main celebration would be delayed until the visiting minister could arrive, especially in bad weather. Often a number of such belated memorial services would be combined into a single weekend-long ceremony called "funeralizing," with as many as six ministers involved, especially in fall, when roads were passable and the harvest was over.[5]

The people of these communities talked freely about death, and they involved children in the remembrances. Widows wore mourning, with a "long black veil" (as immortalized in a popular folk song of the region). Women came together to "piece" coffin quilts and share memories of the deceased. "Grave houses," full of photos and personal mementos of the person, were built, and these and the gravesite were visited frequently by family members, who brought flowers and gifts.

Mainstream culture has, instead, insistently made talking about death a taboo, so that people avoid the dying, deny the dead any continuing role in their culture, and avoid death as a subject in literature, philosophy, and theology, thus making their own approaching deaths "pointless, meaningless . . . and more difficult to accept," according to sociologist Charles O. Jackson, who concludes:

> In this century, at least for Americans, connection between the world of the dead and that of the living has been largely severed and the dead world is disappearing. Communion between the realms has come to an end. It is a radical departure because for three centuries prior, life and death were not held apart. Meaning flowed freely between the two worlds.[6]

The cemetery, Jackson says, is "no longer a bridge" between these two worlds; it exists now without epitaphs, without monuments, without character—an unnaturally green lawn lined with regulation burial slots delegated to what the new owners refer to as "perpetual care" (the very term being laced with irony). What Ariès has called our "death-denying society" has cut itself off from one of the deepest and most mysterious aspects of living, and all life is the poorer for it.

Historical and Non-Western Funeral Traditions

Is there anything you can learn from the funeral traditions of past societies or those of present non-Western cultures? Certainly not if you hold fast to the modernist attitude that Western culture is the peak of civilized thought and activity and that all past or foreign traditions are merely quaint, old-fashioned, and superstitious.

If, however, you're willing to look into the underlying meaning and symbolic significance of these other ways of honoring the dead, you may gain a good deal of information that might assist you in understanding your own relationship to death in general and to the specific loss you are facing.

There is much to be gleaned, for example, from the ancient Greek concept of mourning. When the poet C. P. Cavafy writes that, at the death of the young soldier Patroklos, even "the horses of Achilles began to weep" and Zeus himself was moved by their tears,[1] he's not just using a pretty poetic metaphor. He is zeroing in on a higher truth that goes straight to the heart: that inner quality of feeling (in this case grief) that links the human and the divine. This is, in a sense, that all-too-often lost "bridge between two worlds" that Charles O. Jackson spoke of in the previous chapter. "Good grief" is not just something that characters in a comic strip say to Charlie Brown; it is a transforming experience that involves emotional angst and moral certitude, as the ever-philosophical Greeks knew quite well.

What constituted a proper mourning among the Greeks? William Tegg gives a long list of details in his study of ancient death customs: abstaining from banquets and entertainment, wearing no ornaments or colorful clothes, cutting off one's hair ("upon the death of great men, whole cities and countries were commonly shaved"), shaving horses and mules as well, rolling in the dust, covering one's head with sackcloth, beating one's breast and tearing one's flesh, listening to music "intended to excite sorrow," and a final admonition—"go softly" in life.[2]

With the possible exception of self-inflicted pain (which many societies also practice, from Finland to Australia), all of these cautionary suggestions make a lot of sense—as does even the pain infliction, taken on a symbolic rather than a literal level. "It seems to have been a constant rule among [the Greeks] to recede as much as possible in habit, and in all their behaviour," Tegg writes, "by which change they thought it would appear that some extraordinary calamity had befallen them."[3]

As anyone truly involved in the mourning process knows, an "extraordinary calamity" *has* befallen him or her—one that perhaps no one can understand. Why act as if nothing has changed when it most certainly has? Acknowledging that change, by receding from everyday habit and behavior and adopting an inner and outer attitude of allowable difference for a certain time period, honors the dead and supports the individual who is struggling to come to terms with a death.

Symbolism also manifested itself in the burial customs of the Greeks. The gravesites of kings were inside a mountain or at the foot of one; soldiers were interred with their weapons, mariners with their oars, craftsmen with their tools—not because mourners believed that the corpses would actually ascend a mountain or keep on working, but in order to honor a metaphoric quality of spirit in the deceased: their royalty, their bravery, their journey, their task.

Likewise the pharaohs were buried with servants and wealth, not out of greed or in order to pave the way for the greed of grave robbers of assorted stripes in ensuing centuries, but because they represented order, hierarchy, and kingship in a cosmology that went far beyond their individual interests or importance.

Similarly, consider the allied superstitions of witchcraft and the danger associated with the dead in folk cultures around the world—fears that have led survivors to flee the dead completely at times, to avoid cemeteries, to tie down corpses in the casket, to watch over bodies from dusk until sunrise. Are these mere silliness?

Death always brings life into question, and that duality generates another that haunts mankind: good and evil, God and Satan, the forces of right and the forces of wrong. Modern psychologists and sociologists have thrown out the idea of genuine evil, and with it has gone any notion of real consequence: Children (and all of us) are expected to be good simply because that's the nice humanist thing to do, not because its opposite exists.

When other cultures equate evil with death, we laugh and dismiss the idea. But they are not (or are seldom) equating evil with the spirit or essence of the person who previously inhabited the body in question. That very life (or good) has fled, leaving only the absence of that good, which must be either emptiness (a kind of neutral state that Westerners still propose) or evil.

For example, Rex Jones says that among the Limbu of southern Nepal, "All death is dangerous to the living, especially to close kinsmen. This danger is averted through prescribed ritual." By these symbolic means, "the living have exerted a control over death and reordered the universe by reaffirming social relations. . . . Death, especially death by accident or violence, is the mask of a chaotic universe, a 'universe in ruins.' The death ritual is the Limbu's attempt to capture and order this chaos in his own terms."[4]

Thus, ceremonies and rituals to ward off evil spirits (the

"undead," death transformed into some sort of artificial, unholy pseudolife) and protect the living become much more understandable. The sense of war, of struggle, does not end for the living when we bury our dead.

You may not want to admit needing help, wanting protection, at this particular rite of passage you are experiencing. But whether you acknowledge it or not, cultural symbolism lets you know that the assistance is there for the asking.

Orthodox Jews and Muslims bury their dead quickly, traditionally within twenty-four hours of the time the death occurs. Both groups shun the interference of funeral professionals—especially embalming and public display of the dead—and instead maintain the centuries-old tradition of preparing their own dead for burial, lovingly, as a social community and (even more important) as a religious community. Great attention is paid to ritual and prayer.

For Muslims, ritual procedures begin prior to death. The dying person is turned to face Mecca and is urged to pronounce the Shahada, the affirmation that there is no god but God and that Muhammad is His representative or example among mankind. Relatives are called to the bedside, where they burn incense and pray the Surah Ya Sin, which begins:

By the Qur'an
Full of Wisdom—

Thou art indeed
One of the messengers
On a Straight Way.

and ends:

Verily, when He intends
A thing, His Command is,
"Be", and it is!

So glory to Him
In Whose hands is
The dominion of all things:
And to Him will ye
Be all brought back.5

At the moment of death, it is recommended that the eyelids be closed with the words: "In the name of God and of Islam, the religion of His messenger." The whole body is then covered before it can be kissed by the family.

After these personal good-byes, the cover is removed and a strictly prescribed washing ceremony occurs; like most of the funeral ritual, it is considered a duty of the whole community. ("It must be done even by one person, or all of them are sinners."6) Men must wash a dead man; women, a dead woman. If that is not possible, a husband or other male relative may wash the dead woman; a wife or other female relative may wash the dead man.

The washing of various sections of the body should be done in sequences of three, following the same general prescriptions of *wudu*, the ablution a Muslim performs for daily prayers. Soap should be used to cleanse the body, and camphor or something camphor scented should be employed for the last cleansing.

The body is then shrouded in three garments of varying lengths made of clean white fabric (silk should not be used for men), and the *janaza* (funeral) prayer is recited. A silent funeral procession follows the body to the burial site (no music or conversation are allowed), where the body is preferably (at least in Muslim countries) buried without a coffin, on its right side, with the face turned toward Mecca. Often another Qur'anic verse, from the Surah Ta Ha, is then recited:

From the earth did We
Create you, and into it
Shall We return you
And from it shall We
Bring you out once again.7

Muslims are allowed to visit graves in order to be mindful of death, and as a reminder of the life-to-come. However, in keeping with the general principles of Islam,

> It is not allowed to encircle or kiss a grave, a tomb, or a certain mausoleum, with the intent of securing blessings. It is not allowed to ask the soul of any dead person for anything or to seek protection against anything, for this is a sort of shirk (associating others with Allah). He, *jalla jalaluh* (Exalted be He) is the One Who gives life and takes it, the Granter of all good, and the protector from all evil, and He is Able to do all things.[8]

How do you apply this to a universal context if you are not Muslim? A number of points stand out:

1. The significance of ritual, or form, strictly followed, for a purpose, though that ultimate purpose may not be readily apparent
2. The involvement of family or community as one unit in the procedure
3. The beauty and resonance of scriptures and prayers
4. The simplicity and purity of ritual itself, emphasizing cleanliness, whiteness, modesty, and respect
5. The glorification not of the body or of the living but of the supreme Divinity, who alone should be worshipped, all else being a form of idolatry
6. The supporting symbolism of the Straight Way, the book "Full of Wisdom," the dominion to which all "will be brought back," the passage back to the earth from which "We shall bring you out once again"

The Jewish funeral ceremony has a number of similarities in symbolism and actual procedure. Washing is usually carried out by a sacred burial society (*chevra kaddisha*), where men wash the body of a man and women wash the body of a woman. Warm water is used. As with Muslims, the corpse is never turned facedown, but it can be moved onto its side. The body is placed in a white shroud (*tachrich*), which is identical for rich and poor, to avoid distinction between them. Men are buried in their prayer shawls *(tallitsz,* from which one of the fringes has been cut.

Someone must remain with the body at all times until burial. This guarding or watching the dead *(shemira)* is usually accompanied by reciting psalms *(tehillim).*

Funeral ceremonies are brief; they begin with the direct relatives of the deceased tearing the clothes they are wearing, after which the officiating rabbi recites the prayer "Blessed are You, Lord our God, ruler of the true Judge." (Instead, rabbis sometimes tear black ribbons and hand them to the families to pin on their clothes.)

More psalms are then recited, followed by a eulogy and memorial prayer. The casket is then carried from the room, followed by the family. There is a procession to the burial site, with the family walking behind the casket. At the cemetery, the pallbearers stop seven times and recite Psalm 91 from the Hebrew scriptures.

The family members throw a few handfuls of dirt into the grave after the coffin is lowered. Nonfamily members form two lines, and the family passes between them as they recite: "May God comfort you among all the mourners of Zion and Jerusalem." The mourners wash their hands before leaving the site.

For seven days afterward, the family follows the tradition called sitting shiva, greeting guests in their home, where they sit on low, hard benches instead of the usual furniture (mirrors are also draped), share food brought by the guests, and recall memories of the deceased.

The shiva gathering has some of the same resonance as the once-popular Irish Catholic wake, with one major exception. For the latter gathering, the corpse is present in the home and is pretty much the center of attention. Neighbors arrive to present their condolences to the family, and prayers and rosaries are offered. The festivities are preceded by a "laying out" of the dead, which includes washing and dressing done by the family, somewhat similar to that of Muslims and Jews but less ritualized. In the end, the corpse is placed in its own bed, with a crucifix in its hands.

Wakes can, on occasion, become rather boisterous. Not only food but drink as well is brought by the guests and served up by the family. These wakes sometimes become, as one source puts it, "far merrier than weddings." Usually the relatives don't seem perturbed by the shenanigans: "None of them seem to be resentful of the misbehaviour, nor did they appear to take any notice of it."[9]

Though priests sometimes complained of the lack of solemnity, the wakes (which also occurred in Scotland, Wales, Sweden, Norway, France, and Germany, though they were less widespread there than in Ireland) sometimes included much more than praying and keening: storytelling, songs, riddles, various games and sports (especially when the wakes stretched into the following day), music and dancing, card playing, extemporizing and poetry, general roughhousing (including full-blown fights), and even courtship and lovemaking.

In a study of Irish wakes, Seán O Súilleabháin points out that after all the ceremony was "an act for the dead . . . to do final justice to the deceased, while he was still physically present." Thus, there were times when the corpse was dealt a hand of cards, given a pipe to smoke, or even pulled out of bed to dance. The tradition "helped to ease the burden of sorrow of the relatives, too," even though it appears to have caused near apoplexy in many clergymen.[10]

In an article posted on the Internet called "Hmong Funeral in Australia in 1992," Dr. Catherine Falk describes a ceremony held for three young boys in Sydney, Australia. Their families—Hmong refugees from Laos—were migratory farmers. The ethnic minority to which they belong, which is native to southern China and Southeast Asia, has a complex and sophisticated belief system based on shamanism and ancestor worship.

The funeral rites for the boys were elaborate, even in the foreign religious climate of Australia. The Hmong have a highly developed tradition of music and poetry, both of which were employed significantly in the ritual—"an elaborate three day ceremony . . . with further ritual conducted 13 days and again one year after death."[11] A bamboo mouth organ called a *qeej* was played throughout the "Showing the Way" ceremony, which "must be performed in order to return the soul of the deceased to its ancestors' home, to prepare the soul for its next journey into life, and to make way for those still living and those yet to be born." The importance of the ceremonial words is explained in the dynamic symbolism of the Hmong creation myth:

> . . . Suab, a creator spirit, gave special words to the Hmong in separate boxes. The words for funeral and marriage ceremonies are said to have remained in their particular boxes to this day—brought out only on certain occasions when they are needed and then returned. The words, therefore, might be considered preserved. Another box—that containing words of love and other sentiments—was opened immediately, upon receipt, by curious people. The words spilled out and were scattered everywhere.[12]

Several aspects of the proposed ceremony relating to delayed burial of a corpse and ritual animal sacrifice had to be worked out with Australian authorities. There were also misunderstandings with the local funeral director and gravediggers, who could not comprehend the need of the Hmong families to dig the graves themselves or choose the site according to traditional geomancy:

> We must look for certain places in the mountains: rough, jagged mountains are no good, we can use them but later the sons and grandsons of the dead will become thieves. The mountain to the left is the stronger one, that to the right the toiling one. We have to look for good *loojmem* (dragon veins) for our mother and father because if we don't our sons and grandsons will not be good people. When they die a good place must be chosen for them. Hmong may not be great soldiers or very rich, but so long as a good burial site is chosen for the ancestors, they will be able to live for themselves and not work for others.[13]

Hmong songs for the funeral rite encapsulate a similar need for ritual order in bringing the divine influence and stability down to the earthly plane (macrocosm to microcosm):

The ideals of correctness and conformance to a proper procedure seem to dominate the performance of the songs that form the marriage and funeral ritual which, although transmitted orally from generation to generation, emphasize exact unvarying repetition of specified texts in order to fulfill the requirements of important life and death transitions. These texts have been obtained from a superhuman source but they are expected to continue unaltered through time and space serving, perhaps, to secure transitory and diverse human life in an unchanging and unifying tradition.

The real purpose of this ceremony—and all the others mentioned in passing in this chapter—is summed up by Dr. Falk near the end of her paper:

The longer ceremony provides the soul with ample opportunity to experience its last moments in this world before proceeding to the next, never to return. It also provides the bereaved with an extended period of mourning which acts as a form of counseling for them, binding them not only to the living community but also enhancing their understanding of the union of the deceased with the commonality of all Hmong, dead, living, and yet to be born.

Like all these rituals, this one is a support not only for the dead but for the mourning community as well. If you still wonder for whom a funeral or a memorial service is really intended—the dead or the living—this should clarify that. It is always for both—equally and undeniably.

These ritual ceremonies in other cultures present a uniquely different picture of death, not as an end in itself but as a fulfillment, a resolution, to the overall process of living. This resonance between these complementary halves—the dead and their living, nature and mankind, outer form and inner quality, something here and now and something higher and more mysterious—is what such ritual enactment always entails. Far from being "primitives," members of these cultures may have a wisdom that we westerners have lost touch with or never knew. The Navajo know this, too, as expressed in the following:

> The mountains, I become part of it . . .
> The herbs, the fir tree, I become part of it.
> The morning mists, the clouds, the gathering waters,
> I become part of it.
> The wilderness, the dew drops, the pollen . . .
> I become part of it.[14]

What the Navajos describe as fullness and integration, Eastern religious poets and philosophers have described as emptiness (Taoist and Zen Buddhist) and *fanâ'* or annihilation (among the Sufis).[15] Indeed, perhaps all are describing the same symbolic unity that dying to the world (to the self, to the ego, to material existence) represents, which is exactly why such cultures have so little fear of physical death. These are exactly the sentiments contained in this section of Lao Tsu's *Tao Te Ching:*

> Empty yourself of everything.
> Let the mind rest at peace.
> The ten thousand things rise and fall while the Self watches their
>   return.
> They grow and flourish and then return to the source.
> Returning to the source is stillness, which is the way of nature.
> The way of nature is unchanging.
> Knowing constancy is insight.
> Not knowing constancy leads to disaster.
> Knowing constancy, the mind is open.
> With an open mind, you will be openhearted.
> Being openhearted, you will act royally.
> Being royal, you will attain the divine.
> Being divine, you will be one with the Tao.
> Being at one with the Tao is eternal.
> And though the body dies, the Tao will never pass away.[16]

8

The Question of Cost

Now that you know the alternatives available and have stopped to consider the symbolic significance of the funeral process, you must weigh these factors against one final complication: What will the arrangements cost? Can you afford what your head and heart want to do? Have any provisions been made beforehand?

The chart on the following pages should give you some idea of the range of costs for budget and full-service funerals, cremations, immediate burials (without a funeral service), cemetery services, and the various options (embalming, funeral garments, etc.) and special-circumstance charges (receiving the body from another funeral home or sending one to another funeral home) that might arise.

Keep in mind that these are average estimates. Any funeral home is required by law to give you a general price list detailing such costs; crematoria and cemeteries should do the same. It is a perfectly acceptable practice to get prices from several establishments and compare them.

Unless you choose medical bequeathal or home burial, you will have to pay for at least the following minimum costs:

1. Removal of the body from place of death, and transportation to a funeral home or crematorium
2. Container (casket or alternate) for the body, whether it is

to be buried or cremated (You can build your own casket, even if you are using funeral home services; the cost is then merely that of the materials used.)

3. Permit for and charges for transport to the final burial site (in burials only)
4. Cremation or cemetery burial (opening and closing a grave) costs
5. Cost of a cemetery plot or container for cremation ashes
6. Outer burial container (only if required by the cemetery, and not in the case of cremation)
7. Death certificate filing costs

Any extras must, of course, be considered as additional expenses: embalming, preparation of the corpse for viewing, use of the funeral home or crematorium for viewing and/or use of personnel for services in the funeral home or at the gravesite, placement of ashes by ship or airplane, hearses and limousines, funeral registry book, thank-you or "in memoriam" cards, placement of the obituary, honoraria for clergy or musicians (if requested), and on and on.

What if you're responsible for the disposition of the body and your bank account is almost overdrawn? Some funeral homes and crematoria require payment in advance; others will arrange some sort of payment plan. In worst-case scenarios, when the money needed can't be raised or borrowed, the local government will provide funds for minimum burial requirements. These "public aid funerals" cover only the cost of a basic casket (plain pine box, usually), grave liner (if required by the cemetery), cemetery plot, and opening and closing of the grave. A simple graveside service is usually allowed, but no provision is made for visitation or viewing, embalming, or a marker for the grave. (Presumably most local authorities would pay cremation costs as an alternative.)

To avoid such conditions, funeral homes, cemeteries, and private insurance companies offer prepaid funeral plans. Activists including Lisa Carlson and Father Wasielieski strongly oppose such plans, pointing out that many families have been burned: People thought they had sufficient money set aside but realized they didn't in the end, or they actually lost their nest egg when the funeral home, cemetery, or insurance company went out of business or changed ownership—or when they themselves moved to another locality and the funeral home or cemetery refused to buy back the package or plot. Carlson suggests instead a Totten Trust, whereby a separate insured and dedicated bank account is set up by the individual at his or her own bank specifically for funeral and burial costs; these funds cannot be appropriated by Social Security or Medicare bureaucracies, which as standard practice often gobble up the regular saving accounts and investments of the elderly as soon as they are hospitalized or put into a nursing home. (Another sneaky practice is having nonfuneral-related insurance policies signed over to the funeral home rather than the individual beneficiary—sometimes without the individual's knowledge or consent—so that funeral costs are deducted first after the policy is paid, and whatever is left—usually practically nothing, by design—is then paid to the beneficiary.)

Memorial societies are a prime source of advice for dealing with such financial questions. Their addresses are listed on pages 135–145.

Most funeral homes offer two package plans, one for direct burial (without viewings or a funeral service) and another that also includes embalming, use of facilities and staff for viewings, funeral, burial, and transportation to the cemetery. If you choose either plan, make sure you know exactly what services are included.

When families try to cut costs, the funeral homes can become a bit testy (perhaps an understandable countermove to protect their own livelihoods): they will not (nor are they required to) rent facilities without "staff," and they may try to charge higher rates for some services (such as "receiving" a body at the cemetery if there has been home visitation or a home funeral) than those they offer their regular customers. Check with local authorities to make sure that this charge does not violate the Funeral Industry Trade Practices Rule about "denial of services" and "extra processing fees" mentioned in chapter 2.

Range of Costs:
Funerals, Cremations, and Burials

CASKET

Homemade	Approximately $50
Plain pine box	$100–150
Metal casket	$245–1,000
High range casket	$1,000–21,700

FUNERAL HOME SERVICES

Basic package | $700–1,500*
   (direct burial; no funeral or memorial
   service; basic arrangements, filing
   death notice, and authorizations only)

Additional Fees

Use of facilities and staff for funeral or memorial service	$250–600
Use of facilities and staff for viewing	$250–600 per day
Use of facilities and staff for graveside service	$300–750
Arrangements for funeral or visitation in facility (such as home or church)	$500–1,500
Embalming	$125–400
Cosmetic preparation of body	$75–150
Funeral coach (hearse)	$150–300
Other vehicles	$40–100 each
Forwarding to another funeral home	$750–1,265
Receiving from another funeral home	$750
Package with most of the above additional features	$3,000–10,000

*Can vary up to $10,000 depending on casket.

CEMETERY

Outer burial container	$380–14,000
Plot (church or public)	$100–300
Plot (private)	$1,000 and up
Opening/closing grave	$200–1,200
Grave marker	$300–5,000
Perpetual care/upkeep	$100 per year and up (sometimes a flat fee)

CREMATION

Basic cremation	$200–1,000
Services at crematorium	$100–200
Cremation container (if not provided)	$50–100
Container for remains (family can provide)	$100–7,000
Remains scattered by aircraft (land or sea)	$130
Shipment of remains	$50–75

Estimates are drawn from resources on the FAMSA and IFIC Web pages; Kathleen Sublette and Martin Flagg's Final Celebrations; *and random samples of general price lists from funeral homes and crematoria around the country.*

TWO

Delayed
Memorials

9

Timing, Place, and Participation

If you have decided on a delayed memorial service, you've bought yourself more time for planning and preparation. In most cases, some sort of service—funeral, graveside, cremation commitment—will have taken place at the time of the disposition of the body, but the mere knowledge that you're going to have a more thorough memorial celebration later may soften the impact of that first formal good-bye.

Whereas funerals have a long tradition, not the least of which is a certain public expectation of how they should look and sound, memorial celebrations are a relatively recent phenomenon: In effect, you can make them whatever you wish and need without jettisoning tradition.

There are no hard-and-fast ground rules for such services. They often complement a funeral. If the funeral was a large public affair, you may wish a small private celebration, just for family and close friends. On the other hand, if the funeral was small and private, the memorial celebration may be just the opposite: open, public, with anyone who knew the deceased invited to attend.

The latter is usually the case. When Robert Joffrey, founder of the Joffrey Ballet in New York City, died after a brief illness, his dance company held a memorial in the City Center 55th Street

Theater, the company's home performing space. Any Joffrey fan was welcome to attend, and the theater was packed. In addition to eulogies and poetry, there was dance to celebrate his life as choreographer and company director.

The Joffrey celebration was in the afternoon—a matinee, you might say—but memorial celebrations can be at any time. Theater monologist Bob Carroll was remembered at 8 P.M.—curtain time for most New York City productions—in St. Mark's in-the-Bowery, at the hour he had often greeted audiences with his madcap one-man shows.

Timing should be convenient for those who will attend, especially anyone coming from a distance. This is one of the great advantages of memorial services over funerals: If parents or close friends are traveling abroad or simply live at a great distance, the service can be timed around their return or arrival.

Memorial services are usually held at least a few weeks after the death; they may, under certain circumstances, be held as much as several months later. There are no strict rules. Logic dictates allowing enough time for as many people as possible to be informed and invited. And though there is a certain value in not holding the service too close to the time of death, you don't want to schedule it so long after the death that the memory of that event has faded.

Where should the service be? Obviously somewhere that the person felt comfortable and loved. The above-mentioned St. Mark's in-the-Bowery in New York, one of the city's oldest churches—down in the East Village where theater, poetry, music, dance, and politics have always thrived—has been the scene of many memorial services, especially for local poets, musicians, and dancers. It has the quality of being both sacred and secular, a pleasing space where art and spirit and everyday life can rub shoulders.

Other small theaters and performance spaces around the country have been used similarly to celebrate the lives of actors, playwrights, directors, and other artists, especially those struck down in the age of AIDS. It's important—essential—for the community to come together at such moments to honor its own.

Sometimes memorials are held in private homes, or at public places where the person spent a lot of time—at a college or an alma mater, for example, or in a lodge or club where the person was a member.

If the weather permits, services can be held out-of-doors, in a park or private garden. If the person loved the outdoors, this is especially apt. Those who were fond of a particular sport or activity can be honored in the proper arena.

If the person being remembered was a member of a certain religious organization, the space where that group or denomination meets is often an appropriate place for the service. Having the service in the church, synagogue, mosque, or temple brings a sacred quality to the service; having it in the church's community hall, for example, shifts the focus slightly to a more secular celebration.

Often clergy are willing and interested in having a part in the planning and execution of a memorial service. If the person being remembered was an active member of the congregation, such involvement is advisable.

If the person was not particularly religious, however, or kept his or her spirituality private, imposing some specific religious ritual might not be appropriate. Far more than a funeral, a memorial service celebrates the person and a particular philosophy and way of life. It is not an event to ease the religious conscience of the survivors.

Those who might not want their private religious beliefs made public should have that wish respected in death. A small service involving only those who belong to the same spiritual group is then the best course, perhaps in addition to a public service.

Having two or even three separate memorials is not unheard of, especially in these days of dual residence. A mentor of mine was celebrated by services in New York City, where she lived most of the year, and in rural Montana, where she spent summers and where most of her children live. The two services couldn't have been more different: one in a Manhattan church with stylish modernist trappings and the standard music and eulogies, the other on the hillside next to the cabin where she'd lived, with a Lakota Sioux performing the Native American ceremonies of the Tearing of the White Sheet (to release her spirit to the sky) and the Drying of the Tears (for the rest of us), then a picnic of venison stew among the lodgepole pines.

Double or multiple ceremonies are held not only for geographic reasons or to honor different aspects of the person's life. At times there are irreconcilable differences between those who have come to mourn. Both groups have their right to closure, but they are sometimes unable to share it.

Though death should be a time for resolving differences between feuding parents and children, ex-spouses, and the like, sometimes this cannot be achieved. One of the most common examples of multiple ceremonies is a dual service for a gay man who has died of AIDS, one arranged for his parents and family friends, another for his long-time companion and gay friends. Both groups' needs are thereby addressed.

Who should, in fact, be involved in planning a memorial service? It's a good idea to have an informal meeting a week or so after the death and invite three or four other people from the following groups:

1. Surviving spouse or companion
2. Parents
3. Children
4. Ex-spouse or companion
5. Favorite aunt, grandmother, nephew, or other relative
6. Best friend
7. Close coworker
8. Spiritual adviser (if appropriate)

Each case is individual and will usually involve only some of the above groups. Use your best judgment as to who really cares the most and who the deceased would have wanted to be involved.

Some combinations may prove delicate: the divorced parents of a child, for instance, or siblings who have been estranged. Some persons may refuse to participate—choosing to carry their grudges even beyond death—but others will be willing to try to reconcile and come together for the planning, in which case the memorial service itself can be a time of healing old rifts.

In essence, the planning and the service itself should be "an open field," as a friend recently shared in discussing the service she had planned for her mother. "Everyone who feels strongly about something they want to bring should have that right of consideration."

The open field cannot become a free-for-all, however. The service needs to be planned, structured, balanced. Someone (or maybe a couple of people) ought to be in control and make the final decisions—not rigidly, perhaps, but allowing for last-minute additions, maybe even off-the-cuff responses from those who will attend the service. But there needs to be a framework, a plan, a direction. It's best to discover that in tandem with others who cared deeply for the deceased, just as you did.

10

Special Circumstances

No matter how you may wish for equality and justice, not all deaths are equal. There will always be specific losses that will strike you as particularly horrifying and unjust, either personally or on a broader scale. Some events boggle the imagination—a plane crash, for instance, or young twin boys riding their bicycles on a country road and being struck and killed by a pickup truck.

Certain categories of death require a different kind of ceremony; some deaths are so horrible that it seems almost impossible to mark them with a "celebration." But here, too—and maybe here especially— full and proper remembrance is crucial.

When a major disaster occurs, a large-scale memorial is essential, for the direct survivors and for the general public, which finds the event deeply troubling on the basis of shared humanity.

In the recent rash of shootings in public schools, everyone is stunned and disturbed, but the worst disruption takes place in the lives of those children who witnessed the slayings: It is for them, for their healing, that public memorials are necessary.

The Holocaust, too, and similar instances of genocide and wide-spread slaughter—Hiroshima, Wounded Knee, My Lai—need to be remembered regularly, so that not only the survivors but the public at large will never forget such atrocities.

The Vietnam War Memorial wall in Washington, D.C., is a place of great healing for both the survivors of those killed in the war and for the men and women who survived that war (perhaps any war) themselves—and perhaps even for those who rallied so angrily against that particular conflict.

The AIDS Memorial Quilt serves a similar purpose for those who struggled and died in *that* war. People who have lost a friend, lover, or relative to the disease gather to patch together memories of that person's life. A photo here, a favorite T-shirt there, a lucky charm— all are sewn onto a personalized panel in memory of the deceased. Then all (or many of) the panels are displayed together, and what was private remembrance becomes public. You walk the aisles of so many dead, so many loved and lost, and a powerful sense of loving memory overwhelms you. Your grief is no longer separate, alone, private; it has become a part of what surrounds you.

That common bond is what unites private and public grief. John F. Kennedy. Princess Diana. We didn't know them, take vacations with them, wake up next to them in the morning. But we feel an inconsolable sense of loss, a right to grieve for them. It's a mystery, and perhaps a miracle.

Some deaths are handled—rightly or wrongly—with great discretion. Suicides. Alcoholics. People with AIDS. (Like cancer and tuberculosis before it, the disease is stigmatized, considered somehow shameful, as if it were more than mere disease, mere death.)

Memorial services often follow this same delicate avoidance, making no mention of the cause of death, even though the alcoholic or the person with AIDS may have denounced and resented such shameful secrecy in life and may have been a vocal advocate for public acknowledgment of such conditions and their impact on a public that generally misunderstands them.

Similarly, the epidemic of teen suicides is met with a wall of silence, of pretending the unthinkable simply did not happen. On its Web site, one midwestern high school cautions: "It is advisable not to hold a memorial service in response to a suicide because the service tends to dramatize and glorify the deceased and the suicidal act. The veneration feeds into the magical thinking of teenagers at a time when they are only marginal in their functioning ability." The per-petrator of the policy seems to have little understanding of the pur-pose of memorial services or how teenagers really think and act at such times.

Support groups exist for all sorts of catastrophes and conditions. Your local newspaper should list contacts for Alcoholics Anonymous (and Al-Anon, for those who live with alcoholics), AIDS support groups (for parents and friends as well as patients themselves), and the survivors of specifically brutal deaths, from victims of drunk dri-vers to SIDS (sudden infant death syndrome), murder, and hate crimes. Internet chat rooms or bulletin boards also provide helpful information. All these should aid you in deciding whether or not to discuss "taboos" in planning or holding a memorial service.

We are a nation of joiners, so the clubs or organizations to which the deceased belonged are essential considerations in planning a memorial service. My father was an avid philatelist and postcard collector, and at the funeral home I was surprised to see how many members of his stamp club showed up to pay their respects. Had I been planning a memorial service, I might have forgotten to include them.

If such a club or organization played a major role in the life of the deceased, perhaps someone from that group should be included in planning the service. The group might want to have a display at the service and be included in the readings or eulogies.

Special services are often held for men and women who work to protect others in the community: police officers, firefighters, soldiers. The need for public grieving is understandable, and a service should be planned with representatives of the specific service branch involved.

Members of ethnic groups will often want to include special rit-uals, remembrances, or music in the service. Travelers who spent a happy trip abroad in certain countries might want music or poetry of that country included in their service. In either case, cultural tra-ditions should be respected: They should not be denied to those to whom they belong or appropriated improperly by those to whom they do not.

When Americans die while traveling abroad, there is often considerable delay in returning the remains to their home. A memorial service is thus more standard than a funeral and helps bring closure to what was no doubt a particularly trying experience for the family.

Similarly, when temporary immigrants die in the United States, their bodies are usually cremated and sent to their homeland; it is appropriate to have a ceremony in this country and at their final destination. (One young illegal immigrant from Central America died suddenly—and penniless—of AIDS in New York City. Fortunately, a circle of friends rallied and managed to pay the cost of cremation so that his ashes could be sent home to his mother; then the group itself had a traditional home-cooked feast in his honor.)

When a child dies—or a young child loses a parent—special care should be given to a service (perhaps a separate second memorial service) that includes other children, so that they, too, can experience death and closure. In their book on funeral planning, *Final Celebrations,* Kathleen Sublette and Martin Flagg give the following example of a service (a funeral in this case) for the father of two young boys, to which twenty-five of the sons' peers were invited:

> The service was held at the funeral home the day before the church service, and one hour before the viewing for adults. Beverly began by thanking the children for coming and acknowledging that Ross and Brandon's Daddy had died. She explained that they would go into the next room where his body was lying in a box called a casket. She added that Phillip would look like he was sleeping, but in order to avoid young children's fear of going to sleep after they see a death, she explained that being dead was different from sleeping. The children were told they could look and touch if they wanted, but warned that Phillip would feel stiff like the arms of a chair. Pastor Pete would talk to them about the death [he told a story about a caterpillar, a cocoon, and butterfly—that "the soul leaving the body is like the butterfly, the most beautiful part, leaving the cocoon"], and it was OK to cry and to ask any questions they wanted to.[1]

11

Spreading the Word:
Not Leaving
Anyone Uninvited

Once the planning for the memorial service is well under way and a time and place for it have been decided on, you should consider how to get the word out to those who will want to attend. Much of the spread of information will be by word of mouth, anyway. But you should make every effort to let those who would most likely want to attend know the details. People can be alerted by mail, telephone, other personal contact, or public notice. Some combination of all of the above is frequently used.

Most people leave behind an address book or a telephone directory. Often there is no distinction made between casual friends, business acquaintances, someone the person met once at a cocktail party or dated for a very brief period of time. Occasionally, the deceased might not have remembered the person whose number is jotted down, and if that person is called, he or she—somewhat embarrassingly—may not remember the deceased.

Nonetheless, in the long run, probably each person in the book should be called, either by you or someone you delegate. Often you'll simply get an answering machine anyway, in which case you can say something like: "Hello. I found your number in John Jones's address book. He died last week and we're planning a memorial service for him on February 23 at 8 P.M. at the fellowship hall of the First Methodist Church here in downtown Akron. My name is Janet Farlow, and you can reach me at 222-3344 if you want any further details." It is not necessary to give specifics of the death—anyone not aware of it will probably call you back—but it is helpful to put as much information about the memorial celebration as possible into the basic message.

If the book contains addresses instead of telephone numbers, you can send a flyer or a polite duplicated letter to those on the list, giving details of the service. Addresses can be found on Christmas card lists, in address books (you should not duplicate the phone calls, however), or on a home computer, where the person may have had an e-mail directory.

If there was a funeral at the time of death, the guest register should be checked to make sure those who attended know about the memorial service.

Next, the various organizations and groups to which the person belonged should be informed; this can usually be done by telephone as well. Out-of-town relatives should be invited. A notice should be put up in the office where the person worked or at the school or college attended (in the case of students or recent graduates), usually on a departmental bulletin board.

A notice can be sent to the local newspaper or to publications where the readership would be aware of the deceased. A newspaper will frequently run a small news item in the appropriate section (business, sports, the arts) if the person was relatively well known in the community. "In memoriam" ads, stating the time and place of the service, can also be purchased.

The second phase of this step of the process is more difficult and personal: making sure the key people in the person's life are aware of the service and feel welcome. This may include people you don't particularly like or associate with: a family black sheep (who nonetheless may have had a warm relationship with the deceased); an ex-wife or ex-lover who preceded you in the person's affections; an estranged mother, brother, father, or cousin; a former close friend with whom the deceased had a falling out years ago and never patched things up.

Resentments are easy to perpetuate during mourning: "His mother never came to see him when he was sick. Why should she be invited?" "Her sister hasn't asked us into her home in years. Why would we want her to come?" "His uncle is a drunk and he'll just make a fool of himself and ruin it for the rest of us." "I wouldn't mind inviting her, but what if she wants to bring her girlfriend to the service?"

Think long and hard about whether or not you have the right to make these exclusions. What would the person being celebrated have done? And even if the deceased might not have felt obliged to make the effort at reconciliation, is it really up to you to deny this to the other person?

Most of our anger at the living vanishes like a puff of smoke when they die. Difficulties that seemed insurmountable become mole-hills. We remember the good times from early childhood, early courtship, an adolescent friendship unsullied by the complications of relationships with the "intruders" who eventually took our place.

You're in the difficult position of balancing, of saying who can and can't come. Would someone really be intrusive? Would they "spoil things" for others? Do you have the right to decide that?

Memorial celebrations are to honor the dead, but they're also to support the living, emotionally and spiritually. The sensibilities of the dead no longer need protecting, but the sensibilities of the living do. It's important to keep that in mind.

I spent most of my adult life thinking I was estranged from my father. Finally realizing this and regretting it, for almost five years I made valiant efforts to talk to him about three burning questions that I felt we had to discuss. All the efforts came to nothing; the time was never right, or one of us always changed the subject when the chips were down. Then one day, out of the blue, he fell off a ladder, broke both arms, and died four days later from a blood clot after coming home from the hospital. We never had "that talk." But on the day of the funeral I remembered something: The previous Thanksgiving, at the end of the meal, my dad had started talking to me about a relationship with another relative that had been troubling him deeply. Quietly all the rest of the family left the room, so that only the two of us were left at the dining room table. For the first time ever, it seemed, we were talking about something that mattered.

Yet because he had not addressed those three questions on my agenda, I had foolishly thought that we had never had "that talk," when of course we had, after all.

12

*Finding Music
for the Service*

On a classic episode of the television show *Ally McBeal*, one of the senior partners at her law firm hears that a favorite uncle of his has just died. Richard wants to give the eulogy at the church, but when he tells the minister what he intends to say in the service—that his rich uncle was an eccentric who hated short people, but what the heck, that's just the kind of guy he was—the minister, who is black, refuses to allow any such description of intolerance in his church. The question comes to trial (as do all questions of life in *Ally McBeal*, it seems), and the judge rules in favor of Richard. "No more of this political correctness," he declares. "You have a right to say whatever you want at your uncle's funeral. And if you want to say he was a bigot, you can."

In his eulogy, Richard celebrates his uncle as an eccentric but never mentions his dislike of the "vertically impaired." Then comes the big surprise: the church choir, led by the rafter-ringing voice of Jennifer Holliday, has prepared its choral response to the expected discriminatory rebuff. "Short people got NO REASON TO LIVE!" belts out Holliday, delivering (short person) Randy Newman's wonderfully poignant and sardonic anti-ode to what it's like to be small in the big world. Within seconds, everyone in the congregation is swaying and singing along (as is most of the home television audi-ence), the minister is grinning, and Richard is able to shed a tear or two for his uncle at last. Words of prejudice and hate (the song is composed solely of them) have been transformed into gospel anthem. Music has saved the day, even though the challenge it was intended to counter had been withdrawn.

Great music always does that. It may contain words, lyrics, a text or context, but it's the music itself that matters. As you consider music for the service, keep that in mind: Music is a thing of power, a way to manipulate human feelings either rightly or wrongly. It can be sentimental, maudlin, angry, joyous, or proud—and it can gener-ate the full range of like emotions in the listener.

Such assessments and responses are not merely subjective: The choice of music can create an effect for a service. It can bring peace and harmony, or it can reflect (and intensify) chaos and discord.

This doesn't mean that the music has to be mellow or tame, or even serious or sacred. What matters is the quality and appropriate-ness of the musical composition itself, and the integrity of the per-formance. Better "Jesus Loves Me" on a pennywhistle by a five-year-old niece than Beethoven's *Appassionata* coolly executed by a stranger.

Here are a few guidelines for choosing musical selections for the program:

1. Respect the taste(s) of the deceased: Hopefully, these did not run to gutter rap and hard metal head-banger music. What did he like during reflective moments? What would she play for friends? Did he play an instrument? Did she ask others to play certain songs or certain instruments for her?
2. Involve a friend or relative—someone who would likely come to the service anyway—instead of an outsider, even if the latter happens to be the best singer in town. (A close friend whom I'd never considered a pianist—I hadn't heard her play in the ten years I'd known her—played a haunting folk melody for her mother's funeral. She played it beautifully, but, perhaps more important, those in attendance knew the song

and recognized it as having had special meaning for her mother; in fact, she had been listening to it over and over on tape the week she died.)

3. Keep in mind the attention span of the particular group of people at the service. (When a cousin of mine died, he had requested that Ralph Vaughan Williams's *The Lark Ascending* be played at his service. It's a gorgeous work, full of lyric nourishment and great beauty, but it's more than fifteen minutes long: a lot of attention to expect from a group of Midwest country folk.)

4. Consider the appropriateness of not just the words or the title of the selection but the musical and emotional impact of the piece as well. Music has its own inner nature, to either calm or excite, soothe or jar. Always keep that in mind.

5. Don't use music as mere background, incidental sound before, during, or after the service. If a selection is worth including, it is worth listening to with the right amount of attention.

The real question is not what kind of music is appropriate: It can be sacred or secular, classical or popular, instrumental or vocal. The question is, rather, how it relates to the person and to the situation of the memorial.

RELIGIOUS. There are standard hymns that are frequent standbys, more for funerals than memorial services: "The Old Rugged Cross" and "How Great Thou Art" for Protestants; "Ave Maria" and "Panis Angelicus" for Roman Catholics; "Kol Nidre" for Jews. Other religions have traditional music that can be right in certain circumstances, even in a Western memorial service: Tibetan overtone chanting; the *qawwali* Sufi music of Nusrat Fateh Ali Khan (though Muslims forbid music at an actual funeral); African and Native American ritual drumming; southern Appalachian shape note singing.

POPULAR. American musical comedy has a number of semi-inspirational songs that work well at such celebrations, especially vocal showcases such as "Climb Every Mountain," from *The Sound of Music;* "You'll Never Walk Alone," from *Carousel;* "Don't Cry for Me, Argentina," from *Evita* (just on the verge of being too literal); "Bring

Him Home" or "Empty Chairs at Empty Tables," from *Les Misérables;* and "Music of the Night," from *Phantom of the Opera.* Pop favorites such as Bette Midler's "Wind Beneath My Wings" and (from an earlier era) Al Hibbler's "I Believe" are also standard fare. But it helps to keep your ears open. I was recently struck by how apt two songs were by singers I've always loved: Judy Collins's "The Fallow Way" (symbolizing her own period of mourning—after the suicide of her son Clark—as the traditional agricultural season when the earth is allowed to lie fallow, restoring itself for future plantings and future harvests) and Laura Nyro's "And When I Die" (with its haunting refrain, "and there'll be one child born/and a world to carry on").

CLASSICAL. Here one needs to be careful with length: A single movement or portion of a work is sometimes sufficient. There are, of course, the classic full-length requiems by Mozart, Verdi, Berlioz, and Fauré. Nothing seems lovelier to me than Samuel Barber's Adagio for Strings, unless maybe the "Liebestod" love-mixed-with-death theme from *Tristan und Isolde.* Then there's violinist Joshua Bell playing Ernest Bloch's haunting setting of the Jewish traditional "Baal Shem." Or the third movement of Henryk Górecki's Symphony No. 3, dedicated to the survivors of war and holocaust. And, similarly because of theme, the sweeping opening moments of the sound track for *Schindler's List;* Jessye Norman in Richard Strauss's "Four Last Songs" (all about death and renewal); almost anything sung by Andrea Bocelli or Maria Callas; and the end of Strauss's *Daphne,* where the heroine transmogrifies into a tree.

Then there's New Orleans funeral jazz, the whole world of gospel (anything by Mahalia Jackson will more than do), the mournful but thrilling women's choruses of Eastern Europe, country music's "Go Rest High on That Mountain" (Vince Gill) and "Holes in the Floor of Heaven" (Steve Wariner). And on and on.

That's just one person's list: partial, opinionated, incomplete. Pick from what you know the person liked or loved. See how it fits with the rest of the material you've collected for the service: the readings, eulogies, scriptural references, visual components. Are they compatible? Are they too light? Too heavy? Is anything still missing? If so, music can supply that lack: it has a mysterious quality that can be added to or subtracted from other components, leavening them, making them whole.

Make a generous choice of selections, then begin to listen to them against one another. Whittle down the list, piece by piece. Sample your choices at different times of the day, in different moods. Try them out on friends, especially those helping to plan the service.

In the end you'll have more than you can ever use, but from it you'll be able to choose just the right final components.

13

The Right Words:
Selecting Poetry
and Prose

How do you choose the right words, in poetry or prose, for inclusion in a memorial celebration? Such decisions should be made carefully; they depend on a number of factors, including taste, propriety, personal preference (both your own and that of the deceased), and the circumstances surrounding the death and the service.

There is a rich tradition in literature of writings in response to death—death in general and the death of persons whom the writer loved or admired. These can often add depth and feeling to the celebration you are planning, but keep in mind that such selections must have direct relevance to the person you are remembering. It's pointless to simply choose a pretty poem full of vague generalities, or one in which the specifics have no relationship to the situation at hand.

Often you can find a touchstone: a poem or prose selection with an actual link to the person who is being honored. As always, the search for this connection begins with memory: lines or verses that come to mind as you think of the person who has died; pages turned down in a book he owned; passages she underlined or copied down, maybe even posted on the refrigerator or pegboard; poems or passages you know he loved or those that simply, always and forever, remind you of her.

These well-loved personal favorites may not always be great poetry or striking prose. They may have a singsong rhyme and meter, even an awkward sentimentality. You must sometimes weigh personal affinity and depth of feeling against the cool dictates of content or form.

This can be tricky. Your purpose, however, should be to honor and celebrate the person being remembered, not to impress those attending the service—or reduce them to tears. Good taste and common sense go a long way.

To jog your memory, or to complement it in this process, there are a number of anthologies that have been published over the years. (See the Bibliography.) Some of the old standby passages can be found in these: Prospero's "Our revels now are ended" speech from Shakespeare's *Tempest*, Tennyson's *In Memoriam*, Shelley's *Adonais*, Gray's *Elegy Written in a Country Churchyard*, and William Cullen Bryant's *Thanatopsis* all contain material that fits most circumstances.

The responses to death in such collections vary greatly, as do reactions to death in life. They range from Emily Dickinson's spunky tirades and Dylan Thomas's angry declamation "Do not go gentle into that good night" (with its repeated line, "Rage, rage against the dying of the light") to far more stoic approaches that welcome death as fulfillment or reward (as in Edith Sitwell's "all in the end is harvest").[1]

Many works of this sort approach death indirectly, through distant and sometimes rather vague metaphors. How wonderfully different are the words of writer Wendell Berry read by a friend at her father's funeral. Berry meets the whole process of death and funerals head-on, then manages to transcend it all:

Dear relatives and friends, when my last breath
Grows large and free in the air, don't call it death—
A word to enrich the undertaker and inspire
His surly art of imitating life; conspire

Against him. Say that my body cannot now
Be improved upon; it has no fault to show
To the sly cosmetician. Say that my flesh
Has a perfection in compliance with the grass
Truer than any it could have striven for.
You will recognize the earth in me, as before
I wished to know it in myself: my earth
That has been my care and faithful charge from birth,
And toward which all my sorrows were surely bound,
And all my hopes. Say that I have found
A good solution, and am on my way
To the roots. And say I have left my native clay
At last, to be a traveler; that too will be so.
Traveler to where? say you don't know.[2]

There are poems about specific deaths may be applicable: those
about the death of a child or a parent; about national heroes (the
thousands of responses to the assassinations of Lincoln and Kennedy,
for example) or common, everyday folk; about close friends or relative strangers—such as the sculptor Michelangelo's "To Luigi del Riccio after the Death of Cecchino Bracci," written after the death of a
friend's friend, acknowledging that he "scarcely knew him when his
eyes were shut . . . he who was your life and light," then using a
particularly sculptural image in admonishing "You, his friend, must
keep his image warm."[3]

Often enough, another's grief can touch a common chord, usually one of humbling vulnerability and human lack mixed with hope.
Consider Czeslaw Milosz's deeply moving tribute to his wife, Janina,
whom he loved "without knowing who she really was . . . through
much happiness and unhappiness,/Separations, miraculous rescues.
And now, this ash."[4]

Milosz's poem ends with the odd oxymoron "And ordinary sorrow." Sorrow, of course, is never ordinary to those of us who experience it. It is, in fact, usually the simplest, most commonplace of
details that touch this chord, as in Seamus Heaney's remembrance of
peeling potatoes with his mother on quiet Sunday mornings when

the rest of the family was off at church—an active nourishment that resonated from "Cold comforts set between us, things to share/ Gleaming in a bucket of clean water."[5]

Frequently—or maybe always—less is more, as in these Japanese haikus, all written by dying poets about their own deaths:

The foam on the last water
has dissolved
my mind is clear.[6]
                    —MITOKU

Ice in a hot world:
my life
melts.[7]
                    —NAKAMICHI

What a lark!
Swinging my arms I set off:
a winter rainstorm.[8]
                    —OSEN

Readings for the service need not be confined to poetry; other forms can be worked effectively into the program as well: a few paragraphs from a short story or novel, a monologue from a play, or thoughts on living and dying from an essay, an autobiography, a memoir, a travel account, an interview.

Someone else's touchstone memory can have a strong impact on the listeners who knew the person being remembered, or even on complete strangers. Painter Harlan Hubbard, who spent most of his life on the Ohio River, first in a riverboat, then on its banks in a cabin with his wife, Anna, summons her up vividly for any reader or listener with this telling detail:

In order to see our way among the floating islands [of hyacinths], I often rode on the roof as a lookout, calling directions to Anna who was steering in the skiff. It made an unforgettable picture to look down on the trim skiff and the wake it made in the still water; and on Anna sitting erect with one hand on the steering lever, though from my elevation only her lovely chin and throat were visible under the pink flowered sunbonnet—the sunbonnet I had seen in a row with others all different in a store window as I was sauntering through the Ohio River town of Pomeroy, long before I knew Anna. . . . Attracted by their prettiness, as of old-fashioned flowers, I had bought this one on a sudden impulse, thinking I might find someone who would like to wear it.[9]

From Ralph Waldo Emerson's essay "Circles" comes a message of adventure in facing the unknown that has a particular poignancy at a memorial service:

Life is a series of surprises. We do not guess today the mood, the pleasure, the power of tomorrow, when we are building up our being. . . . The one thing which we seek with insatiable desire is to forget ourselves, to be surprised out of our propriety, to lose our sempiternal memory and to do something without knowing how or why; in short to draw a new circle. Nothing great was ever achieved without enthusiasm. The way of life is wonderful; it is by abandonment. The great moments of history are the facilities of performance through the strength of ideas . . . "A man," said Oliver Cromwell, "never rises so high as when he knows not whither he is going."[10]

Accounts of how someone has faced grief can open up a similar avenue of healing in the listener, as do these words of C. S. Lewis:

As I have discovered, passionate grief does not link us with the dead but cuts us off from them. This becomes clearer and clearer. It is just at those moments when I feel least sorrow—getting into my morning bath is one of them—that H. rushes upon my mind in her full reality, her otherness. Not, as in my worst moments, all foreshortened and patheticized and solemnized by miseries, but as she is in her own right. This is good and tonic.[11]

Similarly, Arthur Waley recounts a story about Chinese philosopher Chuang Tzu, accused of not properly mourning for his wife:

"You misjudge me," said Chuang Tzu. "When she died, I was in despair, as any man well might be. But soon, pondering on what had happened, I told myself that in death no strange new fate befalls us. In the beginning we lack not life only, but form. Not form only, but spirit. We are blended in the one great featureless indistinguishable mass. Then a time came when the mass evolved spirit, spirit evolved form, form evolved life. And now life in its turn has evolved death. For not nature only but man's being has its seasons, its sequence of spring and autumn, summer and winter. If some one is tired and has gone to lie down, we do not pursue him with shouting and bawling. She whom I have lost has lain down to sleep for a while in the Great Inner Room. To break in upon her rest with the noise of lamentation would but show that I knew nothing of nature's Sovereign Law. That is why I ceased to mourn."[12]

The Sufi poet Rumi echoes the same sentiments in "The Ascending Soul":

I died as a mineral and became a plant,
I died as plant and rose to animal,
I died as animal and I was Man.
Why should I fear? When was I less by dying?
Yet once more I shall die as Man, to soar
With angels blest; but even from angelhood
I must pass on: all except God doth perish.
When I have sacrificed my angel-soul,
I shall become what no mind e'er conceived.
Oh, let me not exist! for Non-existence
Proclaims in organ tones: "To him we shall return."[13]

So, explore your own memory bank as well as the scrapbooks and library of the person you're honoring. See what others have said over the years. Sift and choose. Question and discard. Sort it all out and see what's left.

Then consider how what you've come up with fits into the service as a whole: the music, the scriptural references, the personal eulogies. Balance head and heart, reflectiveness and feeling. Consider time limitations, variety, appropriateness. Ask others what they think; weigh their opinions and decide.

Once your choice is made, make sure you're familiar with the material. Read it through aloud several times. Does it still ring true? Don't try to overdramatize it. If the rhymes or rhythms are grating, underplay their consonance or shift their flow. Aim for the simplest, most direct rendering. Relax.

In the end, be sure to indicate somewhere—in the program notes or orally at the time of recitation—the sources of your readings. Others at the service may be interested in knowing where to find the material. And though no formal permission or copyright acknowledgment is required, common courtesy demands a general acknowledgment of authorship.

At the actual moment of the reading, come back to the reason you chose the selection in the first place. Recall the process you've been through in deciding to include it, and remember why you're there in the first place. Then there will be no question of sincerity, appropriateness, or taste, for the material has already been examined, in depth, and has passed the test.

14

Writing Eulogies

Readings of poetry and prose are integral elements of a memorial celebration, but they need to be supplemented by individual eulogies: private recollections of the person by those who knew him or her best. If you (or others) can manage the difficult task of putting your own thoughts and feelings about this person into words—and speaking those words in public—the result can be much more personal than any reading or scriptural quote, which, at its most articulate or appropriate, necessarily remains a secondhand response to the situation.

Eulogies can be delivered either impromptu or from a written text or notes. A service can feature one eulogy or several, from various friends and family members. Short remembrances can also be mixed in with musical selections and readings of poetry or scripture. In addition to the formal eulogies by persons listed on the program, often there is a segment near the end of the service during which those attending are invited to come up and say a few words about the deceased.

What should a eulogy contain? The best tend to incorporate one or more of the following suggestions:

1. Focus on a specific anecdote that reveals a salient aspect of the person's personality, either private or public.

2. Bring some humor and humanity into what is often a rather somber—and occasionally too somber—affair.

3. Assess or sum up the career or life of the person being honored in as full a way as possible. Some of those in attendance may have known the deceased only as a golf partner or a member of a church congregation, not knowing other aspects of her life or his specific talents, hobbies, and interests.

4. Quote the person being honored directly, if possible, from a conversation, a letter, a written account that is left behind.

5. Jog the memories of those in attendance to recall their own special memories of the person. Select a few details and impressions that made a particular impact on you: More than likely these will start a chain reaction in other listeners.

6. Use good taste, out of respect to the deceased and the family and friends, but don't portray the person as someone she was not or he would never have pretended to be. This can be especially touchy when someone has died of a disease such as alcoholism, committed suicide, or met with a violent death. Should mention be made of the manner in which the person died? Can this be done subtly, without turning the grief into a tirade of blame against the cause of death (or even, perhaps unconsciously, against some aspect of the lifestyle of the deceased)?

7. Maintain a delicate balance between the specific and the general, the public and the private, the humorous and the serious, the sacred and the profane. Let people be remembered as who they really were, not as who the eulogist wanted them to be.

Who should write or speak a eulogy? What limits should there be? This is a dilemma at times for those planning the service. You want to be open, to allow as many people as possible to express their feelings, but you need to avoid any excess of sentimentality or hint of self-serving aggrandizement on the part of those delivering the eulogies. Will the person use the event for spiritual or political grandstanding that might be entirely inappropriate to the occasion?

The person presenting a eulogy (especially if it is the only eulogy) should know the deceased well. Often a member of the local clergy or another well-known local figure is chosen because his or her name appears to lend a certain clout to the service. But if the person knew the deceased only casually or briefly (as is often the case when clergy are transferred frequently in small parishes or churches), the appropriateness of the remarks could be tenuous at best. An attempt should be made if at all possible, to bring back the priest or preacher (or other spiritual leader) to whom the person felt closest—or find an alternative. A longtime friend who is a member of the religious congregation could be a better choice than a new minister.

Because most memorial services—in contrast to funerals—take place from several weeks to a year after the death of the person being honored, the eulogist has time to collect his or her thoughts or sort through emotions. Most eulogies remain deeply personal statements—no matter what oral or written form they take—and additional time to reflect allows the eulogist to encapsulate a life in a few words: to pare down the excesses of feelings or details to just those that really capture the person as fully yet as concisely as possible.

What you are seeking is a unique moment to celebrate: some special anecdote about the person that reveals an aspect that you and you alone knew best. This may be why, as Phyllis Theroux points out in her helpful compendium, *The Book of Eulogies: A Collection of Memorial Tributes, Poetry, Essays, and Letters of Condolence,* eulogies are almost always dual portraits, usually revealing something about the eulogist as well, often a common bond with the deceased.[1] What you are really after, in the end, are not details but essence—the soul behind the details. Something like the special quality that William Faulkner attributes to Dilsey in *The Sound and the Fury,* summing up all that she signifies in two short words: "They endure." He leaves the "they" intentionally mysterious. Who? Southern blacks? Black women? Servants? Or simply Dilsey herself, with all her personal/universal qualities.

When a well-known publishing executive died in a tragic fire, her friends and colleagues filled a large auditorium to celebrate her memory. There were many eulogies recalling how bright and vivid she had been as a personality. Everyone seemed to remember the striking colors of her matched outfits. One author put it succinctly: "She lived her life in Technicolor, while most of us live ours in black-and-white." The image summed up the life of a someone who proved (as someone else said after the service), "it's not how long you live, but how you live" that matters.

Eulogies have a way of revealing insights about the person who's being remembered. More than any critic or theologian who has tried to explain Emily Dickinson's relationship with God in her poems, her sister-in-law Susan Gilbert Dickinson, in a newspaper obituary, cuts straight to the core of the woman she knew as family: "To her, life was rich, and all aglow with God and immortality. With no creed, no formulated faith, hardly knowing the names of dogmas, she walked this life with the gentleness and reverence of old saints, with the firm step of martyrs who sing while they suffer."[2] Likewise, Eugene McCarthy recognizes that his fellow U.S. Senator Hubert Humphrey often blundered into brilliance when he spoke extemporaneously: "Hubert liked words and language. In speech, he was something like a jazz trumpet player. He would go along rather quietly, with little inspiration, then inspiration would come. What he would then say sometimes surprised even Hubert."[3] Former British Prime Minister Winston Churchill had an uncanny understanding of another lonely thinker, T. E. Lawrence (Lawrence of Arabia), despite their political and personal differences:

The world feels not without a certain apprehension that here is someone outside its jurisdiction; someone before whom its allurements may be spread in vain; someone strangely enfranchised, untamed, untrammeled by convention, moving independently of the ordinary currents of human action; a being, readily capable of violent revolt or supreme sacrifice; a man, solitary, austere, to whom existence is no more than a duty, yet a duty to be faithfully discharged. He was indeed a dweller upon the mountaintops where the air is cold, crisp, and rarefied, and where the view on clear days commands all the kingdoms of the world and the glory of them.[4]

Ralph Waldo Emerson remembered Henry David Thoreau as "one who chose wisely, no doubt, for himself to be a bachelor of thought and nature" and recalls appropriate quotes: "When asked at a table what dish he preferred, he answered, 'the nearest'"; distraught at the devastation by loggers to his beloved Maine woods, Thoreau said, "Thank God, they cannot cut down the clouds."[5] Leon Joseph Cardinal Suenens succinctly sums up Pope John XXIII as a "humble, familiar everyday sun, which is simply there in place, always true to itself even when veiled by a cloud—a sun which one hardly notices, so certain of its presence."[6]

Helen Keller, who first met the writer Samuel Clemens (Mark Twain) when she was fourteen years old, wrote a eulogy to him some two decades later and described a person only she could have known:

To one hampered and circumscribed as I am, it was a wonderful experience to have a friend like Mr. Clemens. I recall many talks with him about human affairs. He never made me feel that my opinions were worthless, as so many people do. He knew that we do not think with eyes and ears, and that our capacity for thought is not measured by five senses. He kept me always in mind while he talked and he treated me like a competent human being. That is why I loved him.

Perhaps my strongest impression of him was that of sorrow. There was about him the air of one who had suffered greatly. Whenever I touched his face, his expression was sad, even when he was telling a funny story. He smiled, not with the mouth but with his mind—a gesture of the soul rather than of the face. His voice was truly wonderful. To my touch, it was deep, resonant. He held the power of modulating it so as to suggest the most delicate shades of meaning, and he spoke so deliberately that I could get almost every word with my fingers on his lips. Ah, how sweet and poignant the memory of his soft, slow speech playing over my listening fingers. His words seemed to take strange, lovely shapes on my hands.[7]

Eulogies fall into many categories. Students remember teachers; wives remember husbands and vice versa; sons and daughters remember fathers and mothers; politicians, religious leaders, artists, writers, and musicians remember one another. William Stafford's son Kim relates how he awoke at his father's home (shortly after the elder Stafford's death) at exactly 4 A.M., "his customary writing time."[8] Without hyperbole, W. H. Auden describes the day when fellow poet William Butler Yeats died: "A few thousand will think of this day/As one thinks of a day when one did something slightly unusual."[9] Even the *New York Times,* ever so staid and objective, personalized its editorial-obituary of singer Marian Anderson to an exceptional degree: "To hear Marian Anderson sing in person was to marvel not only at her vocal mastery but also at the total focus of the singer on her art, shutting out the world as though she hadn't shaken it with her achievements. What a sound, what a presence, what a moment for American music."[10]

Robert F. Kennedy quotes Aeschylus in his eulogy to the Reverend Martin Luther King: "In our sleep pain which cannot forget falls drop by drop upon the heart until, in our despair, against our will, comes wisdom through the awful grace of God."[11] King himself quoted another master playwright, William Shakespeare, when he delivered one of the great eulogies of modern times to four young girls killed in a bombing at a church in Birmingham, Alabama, in 1963:

May I now say a word to you, the members of the bereaved families. It is almost impossible to say anything that can console you at this difficult hour. . . . But I hope you can find a little consolation from the universality of this experience. Death comes to every individual. There is an amazing democracy about death. It is not aristocracy for some of the people, but a democracy for all of the people. Kings die and beggars die; rich men die and poor men die; old people die and young people die; death comes to the innocent and it comes to the guilty. Death is the irreducible common denominator of all men.

I hope you can find some consolation from Christianity's affirmation that death is not the end. Death is not a period that ends the great sentence of life, but a comma that punctuates it to more lofty significance. Death is not a blind alley that leads the human race into a state of nothingness, but an open door which leads man into life eternal. Let this daring faith, this great invincible surmise, be your sustaining power during these trying days.

Your children did not live long, but they lived well. The quantity of their lives was disturbingly small, but the quality of their lives was magnificently big. . . .

Shakespeare had Horatio utter some beautiful words over the dead body of Hamlet. I paraphrase these words today as I stand over the last remains of these lovely girls.

"Good night, sweet princesses; may the flight of angels take thee to the eternal rest."[12]

When Dr. King's eulogist, Bobby Kennedy, was himself struck down by an assassin's bullet, many of those who remembered him focused not on pain or despair but on hope, as Kennedy and King had in their own lives. Even on the twenty-fifth anniversary of Kennedy's killing, hope was still the message that Mario Cuomo chose in his speech to commemorate him:

After the assassination, Norman Cousins wrote that "none of the attempts to define the meaning of his life said it better than the quiet presence of hundreds of thousands of people who waited in line in New York City through most of the night and day for a chance to file past a flag-draped coffin. Robert Kennedy's meaning for these people was hope. He had recaptured hope in situations where it had been broken down so often it had nearly ceased to exist."

Twenty-five years later, we owe it to his memory to find that hope once more, and nourish it, and make it bright again. To make sure that the "last campaign," no matter how long it has been delayed, is not a lost campaign after all.

Let's listen to his speeches again. Let's read them again. Let's study his words again, let's remember what made him so effective, and let's for once—just once—try applying his ideas, and see what happens.

Surely it would be a better world, and then, by having made his words real, we will have given Robert Kennedy the best memorial of all.[13]

Eulogies can take various forms: a short speech or essay, a letter, a poem. The form will usually present itself as you ponder your memories, recalling key scenes, conversations, or images. When a friend and mentor of mine died after a brief bout with leukemia, I recalled a last picnic outing with her to a high mountain lake in Montana, complete with saucy dialogue: The scene played itself out into a poem for her memorial service. For another woman, who had been a spinner of lamb's wool and a teacher of dancing, the double meaning of spinning became the central image of a tribute poem.

When psychologist and writer Helen M. Luke died, a memorial service was held at the Apple Farm retreat she had founded in southern Michigan. I drove up in a snowstorm. My memorial poem was not part of the service but instead was inspired by the service itself. It is offered here as an example of how memories, details, literary quotes, and snatches of private conversation can be incorporated into a eulogy:

Exchange

"I knew Helen through her pets," explains a quiet young
Veterinarian to a blond woman named Joy who has just read
Two moving tributes to her mother-in-law, whom we've all come
Here to honor. Nearby a writer chats with a man who moved
To Michigan to make Mennonite furniture. Helen has touched
Us all, from so many paths and vocations, with her words, her
Smile, her warm hospitality and her graceful gift of exchange.
Without her urging, I would never have made the journey with
Callanish, the golden eagle who escaped from a London zoo and

Flew home to an island north of Scotland: that literary trek, plus
Those into the complex-labyrinth novels of Charles Williams.
I would have been the poorer, too, without her stories, her own
Retellings of the age-old tales of wisdom, always with a twinkle
In her eye as she pointed out the meaning of carefully chosen
Words (her *American Heritage Dictionary* always close at hand).
Mentor, counselor, mediator between the refuge of Apple Farm
And the rushing traffic of the Interstate thirty miles south, Helen
Treated each client, visitor, correspondent with a precise
And heartfelt balance of encouragement and gentle suggestion.
After reading a book I'd done, she promptly wrote to say: "I have
Several thoughts and should be very grateful to be able to share
Them with you." Helen knew well that books are thoughts we
Share, not reviews and sales: No response has meant more. That
Letter came in August; in October Helen turned ninety, at a party
Here in this same Round House where her friends came today
In late January, to celebrate her passing on the Feast of Epiphany.
She picked the day of her death, we're all quite sure, just as her
Gentle guidance was evident in the poems and readings that were
Chosen today: Marguerite Yourcenar, Thomas Merton,
Homer's *Odyssey*, Ramana Maharshi, Shakespeare and Dante,
Of course, and T. S. Eliot's own Magi poem ("and a hard time
We had of it, too"), then the closing of *Oedipus at Colonnus,*
Which had been read at her ninetieth birthday as well. Like the
Magi, who arrived wondering "were we led all that way for
Birth or Death?" we've come from near and far to celebrate
More than a mere event. In spite of the snow and ice outside,
The Round House is full. "You must bring the pot to the kettle,
Not the kettle to the pot," Helen once said, explaining how
To make a good cup of tea. Remembering that, we gather our
Selves together for one last exchange: here, after Epiphany* at last.

*"A condition of complete simplicity/(Costing not less than everything)"
                    —T. S. ELIOT, "LITTLE GIDDING"

15

Choosing Spiritual or Scriptural References

Sacred texts or other scriptural references lend a note of formality and a tone of reverence or inspiration to the memorial service. They can be chosen for various reasons:

1. To bring spiritual or emotional comfort to those in attendance
2. To link the individual death—and life in general—to something higher and more purposeful than everyday existence
3. To put the event into the context of a specific tradition, a kind of broad cultural or religious framework
4. To add sheer beauty and power to the service

The fourth point—adding the beauty and power of the language of specific sacred texts and spiritual writings in general—is especially important. Because of this, the texts and the specific versions or translations need to be chosen with care.

Selections from the Jewish and Muslim scriptures—the Hebrew Bible and the Qur'an—are often read first in the original Hebrew and Arabic, to render their full poetic range and efficacy; English translations can then be appended for those in the audience who don't speak the traditional languages.

For Christian texts, Old and New Testament alike, many listeners continue to favor the King James Version, all revisions, updatings, and "politically correct" modernizations aside. If the deceased had a stated preference for one of the newer editions, honor that wish. If not, try out a simple test before choosing which edition to quote: Look up the Twenty-third Psalm in the revised translation and compare it to this:

> The Lord is my shepherd; I shall not want.
> He maketh me to lie down in green pastures: He leadeth me
> 　　beside the still waters.
> He restoreth my soul: He leadeth me in the paths of righteousness
> 　　for His name's sake.
> Yea, though I walk through the valley of the shadow of death, I
> 　　will fear no evil: for Thou art with me; Thy rod and Thy staff
> 　　they comfort me.
> Thou preparest a table before me in the presence of mine enemies:
> 　　Thou anointest my head with oil; my cup runneth over.
> Surely goodness and mercy shall follow me all the days of my life;
> 　　and I will dwell in the house of the Lord for ever.

Choice of scriptural or spiritual references is a matter of personal taste and appropriateness, like other aspects of the memorial service. The specific religious path of the deceased should be respected, but the service should not become a forum for a particular religious perspective. The great passages in all systems of belief tend to have a universal appeal that can be applicable to almost any situation. Most such scriptural passages have nothing whatsoever to do with dogma or exclusive salvation but focus rather on universal truths and the comfort that can be gained from various sources: fellowship, shared experience, nature, the passage of time, the common struggle of existence. From Ecclesiastes:

To every thing there is a season, and a time to every purpose
  under the heaven:
A time to be born, and a time to die; a time to plant, and a time
  to pluck up that which is planted;
A time to kill, and a time to heal; a time to break down, and a
  time to build up;
A time to weep, and a time to laugh; a time to mourn, and a time
  to dance;
A time to cast away stones, and a time to gather stones together; a
  time to embrace; and a time to refrain from embracing;
A time to get, and a time to lose; a time to keep, and a time to
  cast away;
A time to rend, and a time to sew; a time to keep silence, and a
  time to speak;
A time to love, and a time to hate; a time of war, and a time of
  peace. . . .
I know that whatsoever God doeth, it shall be so for ever: nothing
  can be put to it, nor any thing taken from it; and God doeth
  it, that men should fear before Him.
That which hath been is now; and that which is to be hath
  already been; and God requireth that which is past.

In a similar vein but from a different tradition, from the text
Atmabôdha (Self-Knowledge) by the Hindu master of Advaita
Vedanta, Shankaracharya (A.D. 788–820):

I am free from changes such as birth, thinness, senility, and death;
  for I am other than the body. I am unattached to the objects
  of the senses, such as sound and taste; for I am without sense-
  organs.
I am free from sorrow, attachment, malice, and fear; for I am
  other than the mind. . . .
I am without attributes and action, eternal and pure, free from
  stain and desire, changeless and formless, and always free.

I fill all things, inside and out, like the ether. Changeless and the same in all, I am pure, unattached, stainless, and immutable.

I am verily that Supreme Brahman, which is eternal, stainless, and free; which is One, indivisible, and non-dual; and which is the nature of Bliss, Truth, Knowledge, and Infinity.[1]

One does not have to be a follower of an Eastern religion such as Taoism, Hinduism, or Buddhism to appreciate the wisdom of the Eastern attitude toward death as transition to another state of being, or as simply another phase of the human journey. From the Taoist philosopher Chuang Tzu (d. c. 275 B.C.):

The living all find death unpleasant, men mourn over it. And yet, what is death, but the unbending of the bow and its return to its case: what is it, but the emptying of the corporeal envelope and the liberation of the two souls imprisoned therein? After the encumbrances and vicissitudes of life the two souls leave; the body follows them into repose. This is the Great Return.—That the incorporeal has produced the corporeal, and that the body returns to incorporeity, this idea of the Eternal Round is known to many people, but only the elect draw the practical consequences from it.[2]

Many traditions see death as the end of a spiritual as well as a physical journey. The classic Sufi poem *The Conference of the Birds,* by the Persian poet Farid ud-Din Attar, describes such a journey as a pilgrimage by a band of plucky birds across seven symbolic valleys: the Valley of Quest, the Valley of Love, the Valley of Understanding, the Valley of Independence and Detachment, the Valley of Unity, the Valley of Astonishment and Bewilderment (not at all a direct, uphill progress this journey!), and, finally, the Valley of Deprivation and Death, where pure light engulfs and illuminates all the sufferings of the long journey:

The Hoopoe continued: "Last of all comes the Valley of Deprivation and Death, which it is almost impossible to describe. The essence of this Valley is forgetfulness, dumbness, deafness and distraction; the thousand shadows which surround you disappear in a single ray of the celestial sun. When the ocean of immensity begins to heave, the pattern on its surface loses its form; and this pattern is no other than the world present and the world to come. Whoever declares that he does not exist acquires great merit. The drop that becomes part of this great ocean abides there for ever and in peace. In this calm sea, a man, at first, experiences only humiliation and overthrow; but when he emerges from this state he will understand it as creation, and many secrets will be revealed to him."[3]

There is comfort, of course, in knowing that someone has had what some spiritual writers refer to as a "good death." Such a death is not necessarily easy or painless or accompanied by a deathbed confession or an act of salvation. In Islam and Eastern and Native American religions, a "good death" refers more often to a hard-won knowledge: of self as Self, of the spark of the divine within, of the connection between living and dying. (An early English tract states "Against his will he dieth that hath not learned to die. Learn to die and thou shalt learn to live. For there shall none learn to live that hath not learned to die."[4]) A similar attitude comes from Black Elk, an Oglala Sioux:

It is good to have a reminder of death before us, for it helps us to understand the impermanence of life on this earth, and this understanding may aid us in preparing for our own death. He who is well prepared is he who knows that he is nothing compared with *Wakan Tanka*, who is everything; then he knows the world which is real.[5]

Hindu scriptures sum up this understanding of the personal self as a reflection of the divine self, or the Atman. The Katha Upanishad, which concerns itself with the confrontation of death, states:

The knowing Self is not born; It does not die. It has not sprung from anything; nothing has sprung from It. Birthless, eternal,

everlasting, and ancient. It is not killed when the body is
killed.
If the killer thinks he kills and if the killed man thinks he is
killed, neither of these apprehends aright. The Self kills not,
nor is It killed.
Atman, smaller than the small, greater than the great, is hidden in
the hearts of all living creatures. A man who is free from
desires beholds the majesty of the Self through tranquillity of
the senses and the mind and becomes free from grief.[6]

For Christians, the symbolic focus is not so much within as above
(though maybe the metaphors are complementary): the celestial par-
adise, or heaven, promised in the Gospel of John:

Let not your heart be troubled: ye believe in God, believe
also in me.
In my Father's house are many mansions; if it were not so, I
would have told you. I go to prepare a place for you.
And if I go and prepare a place for you, I will come again,
and receive you unto myself; that where I am, there ye may
be also.
And whither I go ye know, and the way ye know.

This same promise is echoed in 1 Corinthians:

For this corruptible must put on incorruption, and this mortal
must put on immortality.
So when this corruptible shall have put on incorruption, and this
mortal shall have put on immortality, then shall be brought to
pass the saying that is written, Death is swallowed up in
victory.
O death, where is thy sting? O grave, where is thy victory?

All religious traditions counterpose some alternative to the grave,
a state more inner or more elevated: quintessence, pure music, pure
light; extinction, salvation; arrival, return. It is this hope and possi-

bility that memorials celebrate and memory calls down: self-remembering, community, remembrance of God combined into what Dante called the unifying "love that moves the sun and the other stars."[7]

Not all scriptural or spiritual references need to be sacred texts, of course. In addition to poets like Dante, Rumi, and Attar, many other writers or commentators could be used as well. The writings of relatively contemporary teachers such as Krishnamurti or G. I. Gurdjieff can be used in such services, especially if the person being remembered was an advocate of their spiritual methods.

The writings of the church fathers (for Roman Catholics and Orthodox Christians); rabbis and *shaykhs* or *ulama* (for Jews and Muslims); and various Hindu, Zen, or Tibetan masters all abound in material suitable for services. Among the traditional teachers of the past century whose writings and life stories are available are D. T. Suzuki, Thomas Merton, Ramana Maharshi, Ramakrishna, Chögyam Trungpa, Thich Nhat Hanh, the current Dalai Lama, and a host of Sufis from various orders around the world. Writers—both natives and outsiders—recently have begun to explore the traditional teachings of tribal peoples of Central Africa and the South Pacific as well as those of Australian aborigines, survivors of the Celtic and Nordic traditions, and various Native American peoples, revealing other great treasure troves of mythical and traditional teachings that had previously been virtually ignored by chroniclers of the "world's great religions." These teachings are now increasingly available to the general public.

Such contemporary writers and thinkers often present traditional ideas with a new and striking clarity. The German writer Karlfried Graf Dürckheim describes the Buddhist concept of death as liberation especially well:

The meaning we find in life cannot be separated from the meaning we give death. Seen from the outside, death is an end—from the inside, a beginning. Properly died, death is total release: letting ourselves go, letting ourselves sink, letting ourselves fade into nothingness and fuse with the fullness of eternity. And from this merging with the primal ground of Being, which we ourselves basically are, there rises—if we will only let it do so—our true nature. Death becomes birth, darkness turns to light, and, by surrendering the present and actual, we make room for the future and possible.[8]

Similarly, Frithjof Schuon, the great scholar of religions, states in *Understanding Islam:*

The experience of death is rather like that of a man who has lived all his life in a dark room and suddenly finds himself transported to a mountain top; there his gaze would embrace all the wide landscape; the works of men would seem insignificant to him. It is thus that the soul torn from the earth and from the body perceives the inexhaustible diversity of things and the incommensurable abysses of the worlds which contain them; for the first time it sees itself in its universal context . . . and takes account of the fact that life has been but an "instant," but a "play."[9]

The great early-twentieth-century Hindu teacher Ramakrishna summed up our transient situation in a simple metaphor drawn from the sacred Hindu scriptures:

The Vedas speak of the homâ bird. It lives high up in the sky and there it lays its egg. As soon as the egg is laid it begins to fall; but it is so high up that it continues to fall for many days. As it falls it hatches, and the chick falls. As the chick falls its eyes open; it grows wings. As soon as its eyes open, it realizes that it is falling and will be dashed to pieces on touching the earth. Then it at once shoots up toward the mother bird high in the sky.[10]

Whether you've chosen traditional scriptures or modern commentaries, the impact of such readings is much the same: to bring the listeners to a higher level or a deeper place within themselves. The moment of transition, of transformation, is depicted as the final stage of the dying-grieving process (for they are much the same), which

Elisabeth Kübler-Ross has linked to acceptance. The Chandogya Upanishad details it as a conscious act: "When a person here is deceasing, his voice goes into his mind; his mind, into his breath; his breath, into heat, the heat, into the highest divinity."[11] Poet Kahlil Gibran describes the release in striking metaphors: "Only when you drink from the river of silence shall you indeed sing./And when you have reached the mountain top, then you shall begin to climb./And when the earth shall claim your limbs, then shall you truly dance."[12]

The Navajo Night Chant depicts a similar deliverance from the pain and burden of life into a higher state of coolness and light that can still be articulated in images of human happiness and earthly beauty:

> Happily I recover.
> Happily my interior becomes cool.
> Happily my eyes regain their power
> Happily my head becomes cool.
> Happily my limbs regain their power.
> Happily I hear again.
> Happily may I walk.
> Impervious to pain, may I walk.
> Feeling light within, may I walk.
> With lively feelings, may I walk.
> Happily may I walk.
>
> . . . .
>
> In beauty I walk.
> With beauty before me, I walk.
> With beauty behind me, I walk.
> With beauty below me, I walk.
> With beauty above me, I walk.
> With beauty all around me, I walk.
> It is finished in beauty,
> It is finished in beauty,
> It is finished in beauty,
> It is finished in beauty.[13]

16

Balancing the Segments of the Service

For the comfort of all concerned, it's essential that the program be balanced and of manageable length. It also needs to be focused, not a mere hodgepodge of unrelated ideas and styles. Having collected music, readings, eulogies, and scriptural references for the service, you probably have much more than you can possibly use. Now comes a period of reviewing what you have and pruning it down to a service that ideally should last no more than an hour.

Even if you have been planning the service more or less on your own, now might be a good time to call in advisers to help you select what material is most helpful and necessary. Especially if some hard choices have to be made about the number of people who can comfortably participate in the service, it's good to have others involved in such a decision.

At this point, you should assess the following things:

1. Timing of the material being considered, including length of musical selections
2. Number of people wishing to participate
3. Balance of elements: music, poetry, prose, eulogies, scripture

4. Nature of the various elements involved: serious, humorous, sad, uplifting
5. Are any of the selections too long? Too tedious? Too emotional? Unnecessarily controversial?
6. Are there areas of the person's life, or elements of the mix, that seem out of balance or underrepresented?
7. Do the segments add up to a clear picture of the person being honored?

Once such an analysis is under way, you can begin to solve any problems that surface. Make an attempt to get a broad overview of where you stand in the planning: It's not too late to add, subtract, or substitute.

Emotion and even a bit of controversy (assuming the person led a controversial life or embraced controversial causes) can have a place in a memorial service, but they need to be handled delicately. Sentiments and opinions can be expressed judiciously without manipulating unfairly the emotions of those at the service. But such situations need to be anticipated at the planning stage, especially in the choice of speakers and readers.

Occasionally, more people will want to participate in the service than there is room for or time to accommodate. Obviously, not all sixteen grandchildren can take part, even if they wanted to. The planner will have to pick and choose, as with the other participants in the program.

Care also needs to be taken to find the appropriate people to sing, play, read, or eulogize. Some will volunteer; others will be apparent: Cousin Suzanne, who's an expert cellist, for example, or Uncle Dale, who's made a name for himself singing "How Great Thou Art" at funerals and memorial services. Other choices may require more imagination. Friends or relatives may volunteer without having anything specific in mind. These people need to be matched with the material you've been considering. Still others will have to be asked to participate.

Though memorial services (unlike funerals) don't always open with a prayer, you may want to consider inviting a clergyperson to participate. Another alternative is a moment of silent meditation to open or close the service.

If a member of the clergy of any religion or spiritual practice does participate, you may want to ask him or her to read any scriptural references in the service. But it is also perfectly acceptable to have a friend or family member—or member of the deceased's congregation—read these selections.

Friends or family members who are known to have a flare for public speaking or acting are obvious choices for the other readings, especially if they have a particular reading in mind.

Eulogies should be delivered by those who knew the person best, however, even if the persons asked (or volunteering) are not particularly gifted public speakers. Here content is more important than style, and honesty and depth of feeling can make up for some (but not all) nervousness or lack of ease in front of an audience.

If a person shows little interest when asked to participate, even after a bit of prodding, thank him or her politely and move on to someone else. Whatever the cause of the lack of enthusiasm, an unwilling participant will probably be uncomfortable and ineffective in the service itself.

Seek out musicians who knew the deceased and can technically handle the selections you have chosen. (Not all pianists can play Beethoven or Tchaikovsky.) If no one can be found to perform the selection live, consider playing it on tape or CD, or choose another selection that the musician can perform. (If you use recorded music, make sure that the sound equipment is functioning properly and there will be someone present who knows how to run it. All too often this is not coordinated ahead of time, and there are embarrassing pauses while someone fumbles with makeshift equipment.)

Once everything is planned, meet with all the people involved and attempt to get a clear sense of the timing of each segment. Speaking and musical tempos can vary greatly, so have people estimate the length of their segments. Offer to work with the readers, musicians, or eulogists if they require feedback about their participation or want your advice for whatever reason.

A dress rehearsal for such a service is usually not necessary, but each person should have an idea of how his contribution will fit into the celebration as a whole and who the other participants are. You should also consult with them about how they should be listed in the printed program.

If possible, once the order of the service is finalized, you should take a few days to do and think about something else entirely. Come back to the outline with a fresh eye and ear and read through it again, making whatever adjustments are necessary. Then let it go: Don't fuss and fiddle with it forever, or you're likely to squeeze the life out of it. As important as proper planning is, don't rob the event of its all-important immediacy. Let it be its own moment.

17

Setting the Scene: Flowers, Photos, Personal Mementos

Even before you finish selecting the music and readings for the service or line up all of the eulogies, you—or someone—should start planning the physical setup of the service. Details will depend on the site you have selected, but wherever the service is held, the ambience will contribute to the effect. So don't focus so much on words that you forget the setting in which they will be heard.

Just how important ambience is—and how deeply it affects the mood of the service, in this case—is apparent in a statement by traditionalist thinker Frithjof Schuon on aesthetics in general:

> In beauty, a person *realizes*, either in a passive way (by perceiving it) or an exterior way (by producing it) what one ought to *be*, in an active and interior way. When he surrounds himself with the ineptitudes of an art that has lost its way, how can he still see what he ought to be? He risks becoming what he sees, assimilating the mistakes that the wrong forms around him suggest.[1]

Clothing, decor, setting—flowers, colors, objects of art—all can contribute to this reflected inner state of beauty and harmony, or they can distract from it, even corrupt it. Externals *do* matter, no matter how much contemporary society's laissez-faire attitude may deny that they do.

If your service is to be in a church or synagogue, a particular mood or feeling will be built into the space already: the pews, the altar, the stained-glass windows make for an attitude of reverence and calm. Little needs to be done in terms of furniture arrangement or overall decor. A few simple flower arrangements or plants may be all that are needed.

Flowers have been traditional at funeral and memorial celebrations because they bring color and life to an otherwise neutral space. Probably at one time, all funerals and memorial services were held out-of-doors, in nature, where the flowers and trees lent their gift of grace. But most memorials today are held indoors, and you have to bring nature inside as best you can.

The need for decor will be even more apparent if your service is in a nondescript community hall or other meeting place with less character than a specifically religious space. In such a case, flowers or other items of decor will be essential. Though flowers can be overdone—sometimes people seem bent on trying to outdo one another in their display of grief—the real significance of flowers as tasteful indicators of affection should not be too readily dismissed. And because memorial services, unlike funerals, don't invite floral contributions from the general public, you can control the floral statement and keep it within the bounds of good taste.

Different flowers hold different meanings for most people. Roses carry an aura of nobility and, to an extent, fragility. They are still considered the most beautiful of flowers. Lilies indicate purity. Tulips denote springtime or rebirth. Such symbolism, along with the impact of color[2] and arrangement, should be kept in mind as you make your selection. As always, the preferences of the deceased, if they are known, should be considered. Some of us would be perfectly happy with daisies or daffodils—maybe a whole wall lined with them—or Rocky Mountain wildflowers: purple asters, Indian paintbrush, and fireweed.

Alternatively, you may not choose flowers at all, preferring instead only a few potted plants or perhaps wall hangings indicative of a particular ethnic, religious, or national identity. Tibetan prayer flags can be used to create a simple backdrop to the speaker's podium, as could a strategically placed Muslim prayer rug, a Japanese or Chinese landscape, or Islamic or Oriental calligraphy.

What you wish to create is an environment where memory can flourish. This may mean bringing a few art objects, wall hangings, sculptures, or paintings from the home of the person being remembered. Perhaps people could be invited to examine the objects before or after the service. Certain books and photographs could also be included, so that the space encompasses or reflects the memories.

Photographs of the deceased, alone or with others, have a particular power in such situations. One special photograph is often chosen, either to be enlarged as a visual element of the environment itself or printed on the program accompanying the service. In either case, the photographer should be clearly credited, even if the photo chosen is simply a snapshot by a friend.

Increasingly, such services include a photo collage or a presentation of slides or videos of the deceased. The latter two should be kept in reasonable proportion to the rest of the service. They can be juxtaposed with a musical selection or can accompany a quiet moment of meditation, but they should not intrude upon either. Perhaps they would best serve as a prelude to such quiet moments.

Consideration should be given to whether photography and recording will be allowed at the service itself. Such record making is often desired by the family or friends, but it can be intrusive and irritating during the service. It's a hard call to make sometimes between present experience and a record for posterity. Take into consideration the feelings of those closest to the deceased before giving the go-ahead to a photographer or videographer, and ask them to be unobtrusive (no flashes, for example, and as little movement as possible with the video camera). Audio recording is less of a problem, but care needs to be taken beforehand to make sure the microphones and other audio equipment are in proper working order and that there will be no offensive feedback during the service. (Microphones are a good idea even if the service is not being recorded; often eulogists and readers are not familiar with projecting their voices to an audience, and much of what they say may be lost to many of those attending.)

As at other special occasions such as weddings, reserved seating should be provided to those who were closest to the deceased: family, best friends, or those who have come from a long distance to attend the service. Such special seating areas can be partitioned off by ribbons, or ushers can direct people who are designated to sit together (and politely suggest other seating for those who aren't). Those who are speaking, playing, singing, or reading should be seated close to the podium or platform, though not necessarily with honored guests who may not be participating in the spoken tributes.

If possible, care should be provided for children too young to be interested in the service. Nothing is more irritating than a gaggle of noisy, unattended kids galloping through the space and disrupting the service for everyone else. If parents, for whatever reason, choose to bring ill-behaved children to the memorial rather than leaving them home with a baby-sitter, a room some distance away from the service should be provided.

The most lasting memento of the service will probably be the program listing speakers and selections. This need not be professionally printed at great expense, but it should be designed and reproduced with taste and care. Most such programs can be prepared rather easily on a home computer, then printed out and photocopied on attractive paper. The layout can be in a standard letter-sized format or, perhaps ideally, on letter-sized sheets of paper folded in the middle to make a book, with the print running perpendicular to the fold (known as "landscape" printing in computer terms).

In addition to attractive paper (perhaps a gold parchment or ivory granite, both available at most paper stores), an interesting but readable typeface, or font, should be selected (preferably no more than two fonts; otherwise, the page begins to look messy). Elaborate clip art should also probably be avoided in most cases.

The program should state clearly who is performing or reading, what they are performing or reading (so that others can locate the piece of music or literary selection, if they are interested), and what the relationship is of the performer or reader to the deceased, because many attending the service may not know all the participants. Extensive credits need not be given for scriptural or literary sources, nor are permissions for musical or quoted material necessary for such use.

Be sure you spell the names of the participants correctly, don't leave anyone out, and identify the selections as accurately as possible. Don't trust your own memory of the spelling of people's names, and don't expect the musicians or readers to know the correct source citation of the selection they're playing or reciting. Double-check everything. Then proofread several times, and ask a couple of other people to proof the program as well.

Make sure the programs arrive at the place where the memorial is being held, and that they are there before the first guests arrive. Have them in plain sight where people can pick them up as they enter, or have a few people positioned to serve as greeters or ushers, who will pass them out as guests arrive.

18

*Post-Celebration Activities:
Food, Drink,
Camaraderie*

After weeks or months of preparation, the moment is here: Your memorial celebration unfolds. People listen, remember, laugh, and cry. Then it's over. Except not quite.

It's time to end the celebration of the person you're remembering by coming together with the others who are there to share the event. After the formality of words and music and images have set the scene, the informality—perhaps the real celebration—begins.

Again, you have various options. The gathering can be as elaborate or as informal as you wish to make it. Most people opt for a buffet meal, with or without alcoholic beverages, depending on the circumstances and the expectations of the guests. The important thing is camaraderie, conviviality. If alcohol interferes with that or puts a false front on it, there may be a strong case for limiting beverages to soft drinks and coffee.

The food should be sufficient to meet the needs of the crowd, depending on the time of day. There should be enough choices to allow for varying tastes, including that of vegetarians (though meat eaters, likewise, should not be ignored, a fact that vegetarian hosts sometimes forget). Proper cutlery and plates should be provided, even if most of the offering is finger food. There should be salt and pepper, if needed, and sugar and cream if there is coffee, and plenty of napkins and ice.

If a special course can be prepared in honor of the person being remembered—something she especially liked, or something he himself loved to cook—this will enhance the experience. A unique dish will remain memorable for everyone: a special stew, a national or regional dish, a favorite recipe that the deceased loved to make or eat. One very proper southern lady I knew left instructions—and prepayment— at the local hunt club to serve up an elaborate buffet feast for her friends in her memory. "No mourning—no gloom and doom," she insisted. She wanted everybody to get "plenty to eat and drink." And the hunt club honored her wishes royally.

Good food and good company inspire memories, which is the purpose of this celebration. Harlan Hubbard wrote to a friend describing this portion of the memorial service for his wife, Anna:

> Now all moved to the shady terrace and seated in two long rows, began a lively conversation. Grape juice and tea were served. I called Patricia Staebler into the house, asked her to play the piano, I got out my violin and we played, "Bist du bei mir . . ." one of the simple and touching songs that Sebastian Bach wrote for Anna Magdalena—"Bist du bei mir, geh' ich mit Freuden, zum Sterben und zu meiner Ruh" (If you are with me, I go with joy to death and to my peace).[1]

Such post-memorial activities come as close as most people today will ever get to a traditional Irish wake. You talk, you laugh, you cry, you remember. Often there is a real catharsis: a letting go and coming to terms with your loss through realizing it is not yours alone. There are jokes, moments of levity, which you had begun to think you might never regain. Even a kind of silliness, a foolish simplicity, has its place. After the tension of all the time spent planning the service, it's a wonderful feeling to let go, relax, enjoy.

Even this should come in moderation, however. You needn't go overboard, even in relaxing. Just as you've avoided overindulging your grief, don't overindulge your relief.

Look instead at what you have to offer in this celebration, and what others have to offer as well. The person you are here to remember was special indeed. Sharing that realization with others in no way diminishes it.

The morning after, or during the cleanup, allow yourself to take stock of what you've actually done in the process you've undergone.

1. You took responsibility for remembering and honoring someone else's life, which is no small task. It took a lot of effort, but it never seemed unnecessarily difficult. It came naturally, for, as in the Golden Rule, you were simply doing for someone else what he or she would probably have done for you.

2. You took the time to figure out who someone really was: a man or woman you thought you knew perfectly but who never ceased to surprise you the more you actually learned. The process of discovery was rather extraordinary—piecing together these constituent parts of a person's life—but you barely seemed to notice the complexity, so fascinating was the pattern of the collage you were assembling.

3. You searched for words—your own and those of others—to describe and pay homage to the person you loved. Along the way, you discovered something about words themselves—and music and images—and how you can and should use them with more care, more precision, in addressing the world.

4. You learned to organize and balance a collection of memories to present a single—albeit multilayered—portrait of a person, so that others could understand and appreciate what you arrived at without taking the same meandering, circuitous route.

5. You've come to realize that the person you struggled with most on this journey was not your lost friend but yourself.

You've come to appreciate that perhaps unfamiliar companion in a new and deeper way. You even rather like her or him—yourself—at long last.

6. Death, grief, loss have been transcended, almost without being directly confronted or addressed. By celebrating this single life, you have begun to confront your own mortality as well. And the hours, days, weeks, months of your life have taken on a whole new significance. You see yourself and the world around you differently now—with a new sense of clarity—because of admitting that you, too, are going to die. And through all this you have gotten in touch with something much larger than yourself or the person you lost.

7. Without specifically intending to do so, you have connected yourself back into life. The planning was much more important than you realized, and the memorial celebration was far more than the sum of its parts.

19

Lasting Memorials

You have made a memorial that will last—in your own memory, in that of others who shared in or observed the memorial you assembled. The real lasting memorial is an inner state, one that can be shared with others but also remains uniquely your own.

Throughout history, people have sought in various ways to memorialize their dead. Usually they try to buy their way to such remembrance, funding hospital wings, libraries, highways, and airports. They build bridges and put up monuments and mausoleums, and a few of them actually believe that people running up and down the steps of the Washington Monument will think of George Washington.

Sometimes such public monuments do jog our memories, touching something deep down that remembers John F. Kennedy, for example, or Princess Diana, or the Vietnam War and all they represented to so many different people in so many different ways. Visiting those permanent memorials, we participate in a shared grieving, a loss of hope and innocence perhaps, but one that mysteriously has a particular personal pain, even for individuals we never met or for a whole group of people who died tragically, perhaps senselessly, in a faraway war.

In cases of group tragedy—airplane crashes, classroom shootings, natural disasters, wars—where vast numbers of people are affected, all seeking some sort of answer to what has happened, the situation almost demands a public response to such widespread grief. Like the memorial services described in this book, these permanent memorials—statues, monuments, chapels, plaques—are all attempts to make sense of death, to reconcile it to life and the living, and, to an extent, to celebrate the potential of those lives that were lost.

Lasting private memorials—those we make for individuals we have known—are often fraught with what I call the Tombstone Dilemma. You know that no monument or marker can really represent the person you have lost, yet you go back to the cemetery again and again to place flowers on the grave. Most likely you do it because you find a certain comfort in it.

Maybe we do need a tangible connection with our dead. If not the tombstone or the urn of ashes, at least a photograph or special item that we cherish, that makes us remember. Even after the service, the catharsis, the coming to terms with and accepting of our grief, occasionally we need some *thing* that we can touch or hold.

Many early American groups of various ethnic traditions made patchwork quilts in honor of their dead. Such a tribute was a highly individual personal statement fashioned by a group of women of all ages, working with one another to piece together a memory of the person being honored: a husband, a sister, a grandmother, a child. The death was individual, but the grieving—and the piecing of the quilt—was communal. There's a meaningful message in that.

Recently this time-honored craft of quilting has been adopted by the AIDS community, who took it one step further and displayed many quilts all together: an extraordinary panorama of distinctly individual responses to one common enemy. It is a quilt of quilts. Other groups and individuals have followed suit, offering similar constructive memories and collective acts of healing. The specter of AIDS, after all, is nothing other than death itself—no more, no less—and the quilts personify the grief and anger of those struggling against it; the quilts dare it to show its face. Perhaps death has been silent too long: a shameful visitor barely acknowledged in public. It's time to force it into the light of day. The AIDS Memorial Quilt is testimony to that challenge, as are many other statements in support of groups threatened by everything from breast cancer to drunk drivers.

But each memorial service—each celebration of a life in contradistinction to cowering in the face of death—is such a challenge.

Stitch together your quilt from any materials you like. Use words or songs, snapshots or drawings, a favorite teddy bear or a baby blanket, sacred texts or profane calls to arms. Create something in memory of the person you wish to remember. Or simply create that space within yourself.

The memorial will last as long as you do; its service will continue as long as it is served. Which is all part of the plan.

Closure: Continuing the Process

As the days and weeks pass into months and years following the memorial service, build on the sense of balance and closure that the celebration has brought. Grieving can be a positive force in your life if you continue to acknowledge it and do not let it take over your every waking thought and feeling. Here are a few suggestions:

- Keep active, but don't drive yourself at an unnatural pace.
- Get enough rest, but don't retreat into sleeping more and more each day because "you deserve it" due to "all you've been through."
- Stay in touch with friends; renew some old acquaintances.
- Find a craft or hobby, old or new, and work to perfect it. It may be anything from pottery to stamp collecting—something to involve the mind or body to help balance the emotions.
- Relax occasionally with a good light novel, a favorite television show, or a jigsaw puzzle. But don't become obsessed with any of these activities.
- Get out in public, but don't suddenly force yourself to be a social butterfly, especially if you weren't one before.

- Take care of business involving the finances of the deceased: insurance, taxes, changing bank accounts or other shared responsibilities to your name only. Transfer (or close down) billing for telephone and utilities. Cancel newspaper and magazine subscriptions if the person lived alone. Watch the mail, and if necessary inform the post office to terminate service or forward certain items to a different address.
- Write thank-you notes to people who assisted you in planning or arranging the service.
- Talk about what you are feeling to those who are willing to listen. Don't harangue those who are not.
- If it seems there's no one to listen, consider a support group, perhaps of people who have lost loved ones in a situation similar to yours.
- Find comfort in daily household tasks: washing dishes, ironing, mowing the lawn, gardening.
- Plan a vacation, but not abruptly, haphazardly, or too soon in the grieving process.
- Collect mementos of the person who has died, if you feel so inclined. These can be kept in a special place—in a favorite book or Bible, in a scrapbook specifically for the purpose, on a mantel, or in a special niche removed from public view. Burn a candle in front of a photo, or just in memory. Place flowers. But keep this activity in balance. Don't turn the space into an overelaborate or obsessive shrine. As always, the remembering should heal, not open, old wounds. Recollection is a balance between staying in touch and letting go.
- Plan a project that will take some time to complete, such as a major house improvement that you can manage on your own, reupholstering some furniture, learning a new language, exploring a whole new area of knowledge, joining a gym or starting to exercise regularly—something that, over time, will produce observable results to you, even if they are not necessarily demonstrable to others.

- Explore, if you wish, some form of spirituality in your life. It may be the old, traditional form into which you were born and from which you've perhaps drifted; it may be a path completely new to you. Read, pray, meditate, practice. Don't expect anything miraculous to happen overnight: This is a different kind of "project" from that long-term one just mentioned. Expecting spiritual "results" is a sure way to guarantee they won't happen. Open yourself to grace and wonder. And just wait.
- Balance as many of the above suggestions as you can easily and relatively effortlessly—but not too effortlessly. Anything worth having is worth struggling for in the long run. So even the struggle is a gentle balancing, a middle way.

Planning for closure is like planning the memorial service: Don't let the process become lopsided. Trust your body and use your mind; don't let the emotions take over or run rampant, but don't repress them. Cherish everything; experience everything. Nourish a special place inside for memories of your loss, but most of all remember: Life goes on.

Two Sample
Memorial Services

MILLICENT A.*

Millicent A., a retired high school English teacher, died at age seventy-seven of cancer. She had never married and lived her entire life as a schoolteacher and part-time beekeeper in a small college town in Vermont, retiring only about a year before her death (far past the school board's suggested retirement age of sixty-five). She was a popular and dedicated teacher, much loved in the community, and her students all considered her family. She was a Roman Catholic and an active member of her parish.

OPENING PRAYER: Father Thomas O'Connell, St. Thomas Catholic Church, Class of '61

OPENING REMARKS: Father O'Connell
No one in this church, or in this community, needs to be reminded who Millie Anderson was or how much we'll miss her. She taught us all Shakespeare and *Beowulf* and George Eliot's *Silas Marner*, and along the way she also taught us how to write ourselves while learning to love the great writings of others. She taught from love,

*The subjects and participants of both of these services are fictional.

and we learned to love the words she taught so caringly. Her classes were designated sophomore, junior, and senior English, but she never let that stop her from telling us about all the other things she cherished: great music, great painting, great theater, even great dance—the last of which, believe me, is no small feat when addressing sixteen-year-olds in rural Vermont.

I recall the field trips she would take us on to "see some art" and then write about it. One was to Boston, where we went to visit some museums and see a performance by the visiting New York City Ballet. I was just a Vermont farm boy who had never dreamed of being a grown-up, let alone a priest, but I still remember the centerpiece of the program, George Balanchine's "Apollo," in which a young god is visited by the goddesses of mime, poetry, and song and is taught the spiritual essence of those arts. I didn't know much about Greek goddesses at the time—certainly couldn't tell one from the other—but in the stark beauty of the dancing, all the dancers clad in glowing white and moving like angelic messengers, I found something of holiness: the first stirrings of a call that was to blossom and grow over the next few years. Miss A. explained the dance to us afterward, and when I tried to articulate the feelings the dancing had produced in me, she listened with a quiet smile, without trying to interpret that experience—which was mine alone—in any kind of rational or ordinary way. Miss A. always listened: She knew when to talk and when to keep quiet.

Some five years later, when that call came to fruition in my decision to become a priest, it was clear to me who would be the first person I'd tell. And as always, Millie was there to listen and smile.

HYMN: "Sanctus," by Charles Gounod, sung by Jessye Norman (recorded)

READING: "Death Be Not Proud," by John Donne, read by Jennifer O'Hara Jenkins, Class of '83

Death be not proud, though some have called thee
Mighty and dreadful, for thou art not so,
For those whom thou think'st thou dost overthrow

Die not, poor Death; nor yet canst thou kill me.
From Rest and Sleep, which but thy pictures be,
Much pleasure; then from thee much more must flow,
And soonest our best men with thee do go,
Rest of their bones and soul's delivery.
Thou'rt slave to fate, chance, kings, and desperate men,
And dost with poison, war, and sickness dwell,
And poppy or charms can make us sleep as well
And better than thy stroke; why swell'st thou then?
One short sleep past, we wake eternally,
And death shall be no more: Death, thou shalt die.[1]

SONG: "Sweet Sir Galahad," by Joan Baez (recorded)

POEM: From "The Phoenix," from *An Anthology of Old English Poetry,* translated by Charles W. Kennedy, read by Kimberly Lucas, Class of '43

Lo! I have learned   of the loveliest of lands
Far to the eastward,   famous among men.
But few ever fare   to that far-off realm
Set apart from the sinful   by the power of God.
Beauteous that country   and blessed with joys,
With the fairest odors   of all the earth;
Goodly the island,   gracious the Maker,
Matchless and might,   who stablished the world.
There ever stand open   the portals of heaven
With songs of rapture   for blessed souls.
. . . .

In that woodland dwelleth,   most wondrous fair
And strong of wing,   a fowl called Phoenix;
There dauntless-hearted   he has his home
His lonely lodging.   In that lovely land.
. . . .

He wings his way   observed of men
Assembled together   from south and north,

From East and West,   in hurrying hosts.
A great folk gathers   from far and near
To behold God's grace   in the beauteous bird
For whom at Creation   the Lord of all
Ordained and stablished   a special nature,
A fairer perfection   beyond all fowl.
Men on earth   all marvel in wonder
At the fair fowl's beauty   inscribing in books
And skillfully carving   on marble stone
When the day and the hour   shall exhibit to men
The gleaming beauty   of the flying bird.

. . . .

So the blessed bird   after his death bale
Enters once more   his ancient abode
His fatherland fair.   Leaving their leader
The birds sad-hearted   return to their home
Their prince to his palace.

. . . .

There blessed abiding   the bird has bliss
In the welling streams   and the woodland grove
Till a thousand winters   have waxed and waned,
And again life ends   as the bale-fire burns,
The ravaging flames;   yet he rises again,
Strangely, wondrously   wakened to life.
Therefore drooping   he dreads not death,
Dire death-pangs,   but ever he knows
After the fire's force   life refashioned,
Breath after burning,   and straight transformed
Out of the ashes,   once more restored
Unto bird's form   his youth is reborn
Under sheltering skies.   He is himself
Both his own son   and his own dear father;
Ever the heir   of his former remains.
The Almighty Maker   of all mankind
Has granted him wondrously   once more to be
What before he was,   with feathers appareled

Though fire clasp him   close to its grip.
. . . .

The traits of this bird   clearly betoken
Christ's chosen thanes,   how on earth they thrill
By the Father's grace   with a gleaming joy
In this perilous time,   and attain thereafter
Bliss on high   in the heavenly home.[2]

SONGS: "Sometimes I Feel Like a Motherless Child" and "Four
Gates to the City," two spirituals sung by Marian Anderson
(recorded)

BRIEF TRIBUTES: Three Generations of Students
Beth Ripley Carter, Class of '48
John William Callahan, Class of '76
Lucinda Carter Callahan, Class of '95

SONG: "Panis Angelicus," by Andrea Bocelli (recorded)

READING: Marguerite Yourcenar, "With Open Eyes," an interview with Matthieu Galey, read by Wendy Dobson, Class of '44

One must toil and struggle to the bitter end, one must swim in the
river that both lifts us up and carries us away, knowing in advance
that the only way out is to drown in the vastness of the open sea.
But the question is, Who drowns? We must accept all the veils,
cares, and afflictions that beset us and others, as we must accept
our own death and the deaths of others, as a natural part of life,
as, say, Montaigne would have done—Montaigne, the man who of
all Western thinkers comes closest to the Taoist philosophers and
whom only superficial readers take to be an antimystic. Death, the
supreme form of life—on this point my thinking is exactly contrary
to that of Julius Caesar, whose wish (more or less fulfilled) was to
die as quickly as possible. For my part, I would like to die fully
conscious that I am dying, of an illness whose progress would be
slow enough to allow death to insinuate itself into my body and

fully unfold. . . . So as not to miss the ultimate experience, the passage. Hadrian speaks of dying with his eyes open."[3]

SONG: "Amazing Grace," by Judy Collins (recorded)

READING: Prospero's speech from Shakespeare's *The Tempest*, read by actor Moses Perkins of the New York Shakespeare Festival, "happily a friend and correspondent of Miss A. for the past 30 years"

Our revels now are ended. These our actors,
As I foretold you, were all spirits, and
Are melted into air, into thin air;
And, like the baseless fabric of this vision,
The cloud-capp'd towers, the gorgeous palaces,
The solemn temples, the great globe itself,
Yea, all which it inherit, shall dissolve;
And, like this insubstantial pageant faded,
Leave not a rack behind. We are such stuff
As dreams are made on, and our little life
Is rounded with a sleep.[4]

SONG: "Ave Maria," sung by Janet Hope Winters, Class of '87

SCRIPTURAL READING: "Al Nahl (The Bees)," from *The Meaning of the Holy Qur'ân,* Yûsúf 'Alî translation, read by Uthman Shahid, Class of '97

REMARKS: I knew Miss Anderson only at the end of her teaching career here in Vermont, but no teacher half her age could have been as wise or kind—or helpful to "a fish out of water," as she once laughingly called me after my family moved here from New York City five years ago. When Miss A. would read to us in class—which she continued to do, no matter what modern educators thought or said—her voice would hum. Each new class would understand why previous generations had lovingly dubbed her a "bumblebee"—not just because she raised bees but because she was a kind of bee herself: active, engaged, buzzing with life until the end, taking from all the flowers she found along the way and generating a substance, a honey, that could heal. Miss A. was a good Catholic, but she was also very broad minded and tolerant. I think she would be proud to know that there was a wonderful passage about bees in my own sacred book, the Qur'an. First, I'll give it first in Arabic, in its full beauty, then in English:

Bismillah ar-Rahman ar-Rahim

Wa 'awhaa Rabbuka 'ilan-Nahli
'anitta-khizii minal-jibaali
buyuutanwwa minash-shajari
wa mimmaa ya'-rishuun;

Summa kulii min kullissamaraati
faslukii subula Rabbiki zululaa.
Yakhruju mim-butuunihaa
sharaabum-mukhtalifun
'alwaanuhuu fiihi shifaa-'ul-linnaas:
'inna fii zaalika la'-Aayaatalli-
qawminy-ya-tafakkaruun

Wallahu khalaqa-kum
summa yatatwaffaakum . . .
'innallaaha 'Aliimun-Qadir.

And thy Lord taught the Bee
To build its cells in hills,
On trees, and in (men's) habitations;

Then to eat of all
The produce (of the earth),
And find with skill the spacious
Paths of its Lord: there issues
From within their bodies

A drink of varying colours,
Wherein is healing for men:
Verily in this is a Sign
For those who give thought.

It is Allah Who creates you
And takes your souls at death;
. . . .
For Allah is All-Knowing,
All-Powerful.5

PIANO SOLO AND SLIDE SHOW: "Flight of the Bumble Bee,"
by Rimsky-Korsakov, for two pianos, played by Justin and Jacob
McNamara, Class of '61

Slide presentation of Millicent Anderson, her students, and her
bees, prepared by Kelly and Millicent Carter Jones, Class of '94

CLOSING REMARKS: Father O'Connell
I'd like to close by reading you a postcard Millie sent me from
Rome in the summer of 1978. The postcard was of the ceiling of the
Sistine Chapel, painted by Michelangelo:

Dear Tommy,

Well, here I am in Rome at last. Saw this little fresco this
morning: it's pretty impressive. I guess it was worth all that time
M. spent lying on his back to finish it. I got as close as I could to
my favorite section, where God's finger reaches down to touch
Adam's. Yesterday we had our "audience" (what an awful term!)
with the Pope. This new guy seems pretty nice, though a bit stuffy.
Wish I'd had a chance to meet the really special ones: JP the First,
and of course John XXIII. After that we all went to this fancy little restaurant 'way up a back alley and had, wouldn't you know,
spaghetti and meatballs. Everyone raved about the sauce, but it
didn't hold a candle to what Anna LaBella—God rest her soul!—
used to make every Sunday. Then last night on the way home, I
noticed all these hungry cats in the alley, so I trekked around until

I found a little store that sold catfood and went back to feed a few dozen or so of them. Think of it! The holiest city in the world (well, almost), and they let their cats go hungry!

Millie

That's it. There's spaghetti and meatballs in the parish hall—Anna LaBella's recipe, of course—and lots more to eat as well. Invite any stray cats you see, and come and enjoy.

DOUGLAS J.

Douglas J. owned and operated a shoe store in Atlanta, Georgia. His death came from a heart attack at the age of fifty-seven. He had been an avid golfer, an enthusiastic baseball and basketball fan, and a member of the Bethany Christian Church, where he was a deacon. He is survived by his wife, three daughters, and four grandchildren. The funeral is at the church he attended.

OPENING HYMN: "Rock of Ages," Bethany Christian Church Choir

INVOCATION: Pastor Alan Wertenberger

OPENING REMARKS: Carla Jones Butler, daughter
My dad—Doug to most of you—wasn't really a quiet guy. All you had to do to know that was be at our house when the Braves were losing or—even better—when the Bulldogs were winning. He didn't get much exercise other than playing golf every Saturday afternoon, weather permitting, with the guys, but he got pretty exercised watching those games, and he sometimes used language he wouldn't use on Sunday here in church. But it was all good-natured fun with him. And that was the only time I'd ever see Dad lose his temper. He never took it out on us girls, or on Mom, even though she kept producing daughters instead of sons. We all played basketball, too, of course, and Dad never missed a game, but he was an old-fashioned kind of guy, and it was never quite the same to him as having a son out there on the court. We knew that and he knew that, and we never talked about it much. And nobody could have been more

proud than Dad was when I got the most valuable player award in high school in 1981, even if it was for girls' basketball.

All of you know Dad as the guy who sold you shoes, and as one of Atlanta's biggest hoops fans. What you might not know is how seriously he took his shoe selling. Once at a state tournament game in the late seventies, our boys' team had just made a three-pointer and everyone in the stands was jumping up and down. I noticed Dad walk over to this nerdy kid from my freshman biology class and start talking to him—right in the middle of all the yelling and celebrating. When he got home that night, I asked him what in the world he'd been talking to this guy about, right at the highlight of a close game. His smile faded and he said, "Well, you know, hon, I couldn't help but notice how that poor kid was walking. I could see right away that his shoes didn't fit. I told him to be sure to come in Monday afternoon after school and we'd fix him up. I just can't stand to see someone suffering because his shoes are too tight. There's no cause for that."

I don't know whether the nerd showed up or not—I forgot to ask Dad about it—and I forgot to look at his shoes in biology class. But often when our team sinks a three-pointer and the crowd goes wild—even today, when the team's not quite what it used to be—I think of that story. I'm sure the boy came, and I'm sure Dad fitted him just right, whether or not he had the money to pay for the shoes.

SONG: "I Believe," sung by Bettye Jo Ralston, choir mistress

READING: Psalm 100, read by Linda Jones Parkinson, daughter

Make a joyful noise unto the Lord, all ye lands.
Serve the Lord with gladness: come before His presence with
  singing.
Know ye that the Lord He is God: it is He that hath made us,
  and not we ourselves;
we are His people, and the sheep of His pasture.
Enter into His gates with thanksgiving, and into His court with
  praise: be thankful unto Him, and bless His name.

For the Lord is good; His mercy is everlasting; and His truth
    endureth to all generations.

SONG: "Love Lifted Me," Bethany Christian Church Choir

READING AND REMARKS: "The Purist," by Ogden Nash, read
by Tony Parkinson, grandson

Grandpa Doug always used to say he hoped folks wouldn't get
too serious at his funeral. And that if they did, I oughta get up there
and lighten things up a bit. He used to recite these funny poems he'd
learned when he was a kid in school. Kids don't learn poems in
school anymore, you know, and Grandpa thought that was "a damn
shame," though I probably shouldn't say that in church. Anyway,
here's one of the poems he taught me, which also happens to be
about dying, but it's still funny anyway. It's called "The Purist," by
Mr. Ogden Nash. I guess you had to be funny with a name like that.
Anywhere, here goes:

> I give you now Professor Twist,
> A conscientious scientist.
> Trustees exclaimed, "He never bungles!"
> And sent him off to distant jungles.
> Camped on a tropic riverside
> One day he missed his loving bride.
> She had, the guide informed him later,
> Been eaten by an alligator.
> Professor Twist could not but smile.
> "You mean," he said, "a crocodile."[6]

SOLO: "In the Garden," sung by Peter McMillan, golf partner and
choir member

READING: From *Young Men and Fire,* by Norman Maclean, read
by Susan Jones Bradley, daughter

My dad was not much of a reader, or at least he always pretended not to be. The one book I know that he loved best was Norman Maclean's *A River Runs Through It,* which is pretty much a man's book about trout fishing in Montana, and so much more. I know, because it's one of my favorite books as well—man's book or not.

Maclean wrote only one other book, near the end of his life. He had always been haunted by the deaths of twelve young smoke jumpers in the Mann's Gulch Fire in 1949. He wrote a wonderful book exploring those firefighters' deaths and his fascination with them. Dad read that book as well and told me how moved he was by its ending. I'd like to read part of it for you here, beginning where Maclean wonders what the young men were thinking just before they died. A freak blowup trapped and killed them near the top of a hill where they were trying to douse a relatively simple forest fire:

One thing is certain about these final thoughts—there was not much size to them. Time and place did not permit even superior young men dying suddenly "to see their whole lives pass in review," although books portray people preparing to die as seeing a sort of documentary movie of their lives. Everything, however, gets smaller on its way to becoming eternal. It is also probable that the final thoughts of elite young men dying suddenly were not see- ing or scenic thoughts but were cries or a single cry of passion, often of self-compassion, justifiable if those who cry are justly proud. The two living survivors of the Mann Gulch fire have told me that, as they went up the last hillside, they remember thinking only, "My God, how could you do this to me? I cannot be allowed to die so young and so close to the top." They said they could remember hearing their voices saying this out loud. Of the two great tragic emotions this close to the end, fear had been burned away and pity was in sole possession. Not only is it heat that burns fear away; the end of tragedy purifies itself of it. . . . The pity that remains is perhaps the last and only emotion felt if it is the young and unfulfilled who suffer the tragedy. . . .

The most eloquent expression of this cry was made by a young man who came from the sky and returned to it and who, while on earth, knew he was alone and beyond all other men, and who, when he died, died on a hill: "About the ninth hour he cried with a loud voice, Eli, Eli, lama sabachthani?" ("My God, my God, why hast thou forsaken me?")

Although we can enter their last thoughts and feelings only by indirection, we are sure of the final act of many of them. Dr. Hawkins, the physician who went in with the rescue crew the night the men were burned, told me that, after the bodies had fallen, most of them had risen again, taken a few steps, and fallen again, this final time like pilgrims in prayer, facing the top of the hill, which on that slope is nearly east. Ranger Jansson, in charge of the rescue crew, independently made the same observation.

The evidence, then, is that at the very end beyond thought and beyond fear and beyond even self-compassion and divine bewilderment there remains some firm intention to continue doing forever and ever what we last hoped to do on earth. By this final act they had come about as close as body and spirit can to establishing a unity of themselves with earth, fire, and perhaps the sky. . . .

I, an old man, have written this fire report. Among other things, it was important to me, as an exercise for old age, to enlarge my knowledge and spirit so I could accompany young men whose lives I might have lived on their way to death. I have climbed where they climbed, and in my time I have fought fire and inquired into its nature. In addition, I have lived to get a better understanding of myself and those close to me, many of them now dead. Perhaps it is not odd, at the end of this tragedy where nothing much was left of the elite who came from the sky but courage and struggling for oxygen, that I have often found myself thinking of my wife on her brave and lonely way to death.[7]

CLOSING HYMN: "Just As I Am," Bethany Christian Church Choir

CLOSING PRAYER: Pastor Alan Wertenberger

Memorial Societies
in the United States

MEMBERS OF THE
FUNERAL AND MEMORIAL SOCIETY OF AMERICA
P.O. BOX 10, HINESBURG, VT 05461
1-800-765-0107
WEB SITE: www.funerals.org/famsa

The following consumer groups are run mostly by volunteers, many of whom are also full-time caregivers themselves. Therefore, in some cases telephone numbers have not been listed and post office box addresses, not street addresses, are given. Callers seeking information should contact the memorial group closest to their own geographic location, regardless of state. Those who have difficulty reaching a society or who cannot find one listed in their immediate area should call the FAMSA office directly. Listings are alphabetized by city under each state.

Alaska

Cook Inlet Memorial
P.O. Box 102414
Anchorage, AK 99510-2414
907-566-3732

Arizona

Valley Memorial Society
Box 0423
Chandler, AZ 85244-0423
602-929-9659

Memorial Society of Prescott
P.O. Box 1090
Prescott, AZ 86302-1090
520-778-3000

Memorial Society of Southern
   Arizona
P.O. Box 12661
Tucson, AZ 85732-2661
520-721-0230

Arkansas

Northwest Arkansas Memorial
   Society
P.O. Box 3055
Fayetteville, AR 72702-3055
501-443-1404

California

Humboldt Funeral Society
P.O. Box 856
Arcata, CA 95518-0856
707-822-8599

Kern Memorial Society
P.O. Box 1202
Bakersfield, CA 93302-1202
805-366-7266 or 805-854-5689

Bay Area Funeral Society
P.O. Box 264
Berkeley, CA 94701-0264
510-841-6653

Redwood Funeral Society
P.O. Box 7501
Cotati, CA 94931-7501
707-824-8360

Valley Memorial Society
P.O. Box 101
Fresno, CA 93707-0101
559-268-2181

Stanislaus Memorial Society
P.O. Box 4252
Modesto, CA 95352-4252
209-521-7690

Channel Cities Memorial Society
P.O. Box 1778
Ojai, CA 93024-1778
805-640-0109 or
   1-800-520-PLAN (from 805
   area code only)

Funeral and Memorial Planning
   Society
P.O. Box 60448
Palo Alto, CA 94306-0448
650-321-2109 or
   (toll-free) 888-775-5553

Los Angeles Funeral Society
P.O. Box 92313
Pasadena, CA 91109-2313
626-683-3545 or 626-683-3752

Sacramento Valley Memorial
   Society
P.O. Box 161688
Sacramento, CA 95816-1688
916-451-4641

San Diego Memorial Society
P.O. Box 16336
San Diego, CA 92176-6336
619-293-0926

Central Coast Memorial Society
P.O. Box 679
San Luis Obispo, CA
    93406-0679
805-543-6133

Funeral and Memorial Society
    of Monterey Bay
Box 2900
Santa Cruz, CA 95063-2900
831-426-3308

San Joaquin Memorial Society
Box 4832
Stockton, CA 95204-4832
209-465-2741

Colorado

Funeral Consumer Society of
    Colorado
4101 E. Hampden Ave.
Denver, CO 80222-7262
303-759-2800 or
    (toll-free) 888-438-6431

Connecticut

Funeral Consumer Information
    Society of Connecticut
P.O. Box 34
Bridgewater, CT 06752-0034
860-355-4197 or 800-607-2801

Delaware

Served by Memorial Society of
    Maryland

District of Columbia

Memorial Society of
    Metropolitan Washington
1500 Harvard St. NW
Washington, DC 20009-4216
202-234-7777

Florida

Funeral and Memorial Society of
    Brevard County
P.O. Box 276
Cocoa, FL 32923-0276
407-453-4109 or 407-636-3363

Funeral Society of Mid-Florida
P.O. Box 392
De Bary, FL 32713-0392
904-789-1682 or 407-668-6822

Funeral and Memorial Society of
    Southwest Florida
P.O. Box 7756
Ft. Myers, FL 33911-7756
941-573-0507

Memorial Society of Alachua
    County
Box 14662
Gainesville, FL 32604-4662
352-378-3432

Memorial and Funeral Society of
    Greater Orlando
P.O. Box 953
Goldenrod, FL 32733-0953
407-677-5009

Palm Beach Funeral Society
P.O. Box 31982
Palm Beach, FL 33420-1982
561-659-4881

Memorial Society of Tampa Bay
45 Katherine Blvd. #307
Palm Harbor, FL 34684-3648

Funeral and Memorial Society of
    Pensacola and West Florida
7804 Northpointe Blvd.
Pensacola, FL 32514-6537
850-477-8431

Suncoast-Tampa Bay Memorial
    Society
719 Arlington Ave. N.
St. Petersburg, FL 33701-3621
727-895-1442

Memorial Society of Sarasota
P.O. Box 15833
Sarasota, FL 34277-5833
941-953-3740

Funeral and Memorial Society of
    Leon County
1006 Buena Vista Dr.
Tallahassee, FL 32304-1810
850-224-2082

Georgia

Memorial Society of Georgia
1911 Cliff Valley Way NE
Atlanta, GA 30329-2420
404-634-2896 or 800-840-4339

Middle Georgia Chapter
5276 Zebulon Rd.
Macon, GA 31210-2136
800-840-4339

Hawaii

Memorial Society of Hawaii
2510 Bingham St., Room A
Honolulu, HI 96826-1539
808-946-6822

Idaho

Idaho Memorial Association
P.O. Box 1919
Boise, ID 83701-1919
208-343-4581

Illinois

Chicago Memorial Association
Box 2923
Chicago, IL 60690-2923

Champaign County Memorial
    Society
309 W. Green St.
Urbana, IL 61801-3221
217-384-8862

Indiana

Bloomington Memorial Society
2120 N. Fee Ln.
Bloomington, IN 47408-1646

Indianapolis Memorial Society
5805 E. 56th St.
Indianapolis, IN 46226-1526

Memorial Society of Northwest
    Indiana
P.O. Box 329
Valparaiso, IN 46384-0329
219-464-3024 or 219-464-5482

Iowa

Memorial Society of Iowa River
   Valley
120 N. Dubuque St.
Iowa City, IA 52245-1708
319-338-2637

For all other areas of the state,
   call the FAMSA office:
   800-765-0107

Kentucky

Memorial Society of Greater
   Louisville
P.O. Box 5326
Louisville, KY 40255-5326

Louisiana

Memorial Society of Greater
   Baton Rouge
8470 Goodwood Ave.
Baton Rouge, LA 70806-7849

Maine

Memorial Society of Maine
Box 3122
Auburn, ME 04212-3122
207-786-4323

Maryland

Memorial Society of Maryland
9601 Cedar Ln.
Bethesda, MD 20814-4045
800-564-0017

Massachusetts

The Memorial Society
66 Marlborough St.
Boston, MA 02116-2007
617-859-7990 or
   (toll-free) 888-666-7990

Memorial Society of Cape Cod
P.O. Box 1375
East Orleans, MA 02643-1375
508-862-2522 or 800-976-9552

New Bedford Memorial Society
   of SE Massachusetts
71 8th St.
New Bedford, MA 02740-6025

Memorial Society of Western
   Massachusetts
P.O. Box 2821
Springfield, MA 01101-2821
413-783-7987

Michigan

Memorial Advisory and
   Planning Society
2030 Chaucer Dr.
Ann Arbor, MI 48103-6106
734-665-9516

Greater Detroit Memorial
   Society
P.O. Box 24054
Detroit, MI 48224-4054
313-886-0998

Memorial Society of Flint
P.O. Box 4315
Flint, MI 48504-4315
810-239-2596

Minnesota

Minnesota Funeral and
    Memorial Society
717 Riverside Dr. SE
St. Cloud, MN 56304-1448
612-374-1515

Missouri

Funeral and Memorial Society of
    Greater Kansas City
4500 Warwick Blvd.
Kansas City, MO 64111-1822
816-561-6322

Funeral Consumer Information
    Society
216 E. Argonne Ave.
St. Louis, MO 63122-4310
314-997-9819

Montana

Memorial Society of Montana
1024 Princeton Ave.
Billings, MT 59102-1838
406-252-5065

Five Valleys Burial Memorial
    Association
405 University Ave.
Missoula, MT 59801-4437

Nevada

Funeral Consumer Information
    Society of Nevada
Box 8413, University Station
Reno, NV 89507-8413
702-329-7705

New Hampshire

Memorial Society of New
    Hampshire
P.O. Box 941
Epping, NH 03042-0941
603-679-5721

New Jersey

Memorial Society of South
    Jersey
401 Kings Highway N.
Cherry Hill, NJ 08034-1016

Raritan Valley Memorial Society
176 Tices Ln.
East Brunswick, NJ 08816-1345
732-572-1470 (board member)

Memorial Association of
    Monmouth County
1475 W. Front St.
Lincroft, NJ 07738-1118

Morris Memorial Society
Box 509
Madison, NJ 07940-0509
973-540-9140

Memorial Society of Essex
P.O. Box 1327
Montclair, NJ 07042-1327
973-783-1145

Central Memorial Society
156 Forest Ave.
Paramus, NJ 07652-5326
201-385-4153

Princeton Memorial Association
48 Roper Rd.
Princeton, NJ 08540-4070
609-924-5525 or 609-924-1604

New Mexico

Memorial & Funeral Society of
  Southern New Mexico
P.O. Box 6531
Las Cruces, NM 88006-6531
505-526-7761

Funeral Consumer Information
  Society of Northern New
  Mexico
P.O. Box 15164
Rio Rancho, NM 87174-5164
505-296-5902

New York

Memorial Society of the
  Hudson-Mohawk Region
405 Washington Ave.
Albany, NY 12206-2604
518-465-9664

Southern Tier Memorial Society
183 Riverside Dr.
Binghamton, NY 13905-4171

Greater Buffalo Memorial Society
695 Elmwood Ave.
Buffalo, NY 14222-1601
716-837-8636

Syracuse Memorial Society
P.O. Box 67
De Witt, NY 13214-0067
315-446-0557 or 315-478-7258

Memorial Society of Long Island
Box 3495
Farmingdale, NY 11735-0694
516-541-6587

Ithaca Memorial Society
Box 134
Ithaca, NY 14851-0134
607-273-8316

Mohawk Valley Memorial
  Society
P.O. Box 322
New Hartford, NY 13413-0322
315-797-2396 or 315-735-6268

Memorial Society of Riverside
  Church
490 Riverside Dr.
New York, NY 10027-5713
212-870-6785 (Tues. 10–3 or
  leave message)

Community Church of NY
  Funeral Society
40 East 35th St.
New York, NY 10016-3806
212-683-4988

Memorial Society of Greater
  Corning Area
P.O. Box 23
Painted Post, NY 14870-0023
607-962-7132 or 607-936-6563

Mid-Hudson Memorial Society
249 Hooker Ave.
Poughkeepsie, NY 12603-3327
914-229-0241

Rochester Memorial Society
220 Winton Rd. S.
Rochester, NY 14610-2956
716-461-1620

Funeral Planning Association of
    Westchester
460 York Ct.
Yorktown Heights, NY
    10598-3726

North Carolina

Blue Ridge Memorial Society
P.O. Box 2601
Asheville, NC 28802-2601
828-669-2587

Memorial Society of the Triangle
P.O. Box 1223
Chapel Hill, NC 27514-1223
919-834-6898

Piedmont Memorial & Funeral
    Society
5137 Charleston Rd.
Pleasant Garden, NC 27313-9231
336-674-5501

Memorial Society of the Lower
    Cape Fear
P.O. Box 4262
Wilmington, NC 28406-4262

Ohio

Memorial Society of Akron-
    Canton Area
3300 Morewood Rd.
Akron, OH 44333-3459
330-836-4418 or 330-849-1030

Memorial Society of Greater
    Cincinnati
536 Linton St.
Cincinnati, OH 45219-2438

Memorial Society of the
    Columbus Area
P.O. Box 14835
Columbus, OH 43214-4835
614-436-8911

Cleveland Memorial Society
21600 Shaker Blvd.
Shaker Heights, OH 44122-2662
216-751-5515

Memorial Society of Northwest
    Ohio
2210 Collingwood Blvd.
Toledo, OH 43620-1147
419-475-1429
E-mail:
    gfulton@utnet.utoledo.edu

Oklahoma

All Oklahoma cities, call
    1-800-371-2221

Oregon

Oregon Memorial Association
P.O. Box 25578
Portland, OR 97298-5578
503-297-3513 or
    (toll-free) 888-475-5520
E-mail: cvroberts@madras.net

Pennsylvania

Memorial Society of Erie
Box 3495
Erie, PA 16508-3495
814-456-4433

Memorial Society of Greater
  Harrisburg
1280 Clover Ln.
Harrisburg, PA 17113-1001
717-564-8507

Memorial Society of Greater
  Philadelphia
2125 Chestnut St.
Philadelphia, PA 19103-3146
215-567-1065

Pittsburgh Memorial Society
605 Morewood Ave.
Pittsburgh, PA 15213-2909
724-621-4740

Memorial Society of Central
  Pennsylvania
780 Waupelani Dr. Ext.
State College, PA 16801-7800

Rhode Island

Memorial Society of Rhode
  Island
119 Kenyon Ave.
East Greenwich, RI 02818-2905
401-884-5933

South Carolina

Funeral & Memorial Society of
  South Carolina
2701 Heyward St.
Columbia, SC 29205-2523
803-772-7054

South Dakota

Funeral Consumer Information
  Society of the Dakotas
HCR 66, Box 10
Lemmon, SD 57638-9702
605-374-5336

Tennessee

Memorial Society of
  Chattanooga
3224 Navajo Dr.
Chattanooga, TN 37411-5036

East Tennessee Memorial Society
P.O. Box 10507
Knoxville, TN 37939-0507

Memorial Society of Middle
  Tennessee
1808 Woodmont Blvd.
Nashville, TN 37215-1528
615-661-7586 or
  (toll-free) 888-254-3872

Texas

Austin Memorial & Burial
  Information Society
P.O. Box 4382
Austin, TX 78765-4382
512-480-0555

Memorial Society of South
  Texas
3125 Horne Rd.
Corpus Christi, TX 78415-5033
800-371-2221

Memorial Society of North
  Texas
(serving Dallas, Denton, Fort
  Worth, Lubbock, Tyler, and
  Wichita Falls)
4015 Normandy Ave.
Dallas, TX 75205-1750
214-528-6006 or 800-371-2221
  (TX and OK only)

Houston Area Memorial Society
5200 Fannin St.
Houston, TX 77004-5899
713-526-4267

San Antonio Memorial Society
7150 Interstate 10 West
San Antonio, TX 78213-3468
210-341-2213

Memorial Society of North
  Texas, Central Texas Chapter
4209 N. 27th St.
Waco, TX 76708-1509
800-371-2221 (TX and OK only)

Vermont

Vermont Memorial Society
Box 457
Hinesburg, VT 05461-0457
802-468-3210 or 800-805-0007
  (VT only)
SE Branch: 802-875-3192
NE Branch: 802-626-8123
NW Branch: 802-482-3437

Virginia

Memorial Society of Northern
  Virginia
4444 Arlington Blvd.
Arlington, VA 22204-1340
703-271-9240

Memorial Planning Society of
  the Piedmont
717 Rugby Rd.
Charlottesville, VA 22903-1626
804-293-8179

Funeral Consumer Information
  Society of Virginia
(serving Richmond area)
P.O. Box 3712
Glen Allen, VA 23058-3712
804-745-3682

Memorial Society of Tidewater
P.O. Box 4621
Virginia Beach, VA 23454-4621

Washington

People's Memorial Association
2366 Eastlake Ave. E., Areis
  Bldg. #409
Seattle, WA 98102-3366
206-325-0489
E-mail: pma-info@peoples-
  memorial.org

Spokane Memorial Association
P.O. Box 13613
Spokane, WA 99213-13613
509-924-8400

Funeral Association of Central
  Washington
1916 N. 4th St.
Yakima, WA 98901-1815
509-248-4533

West Virginia

Memorial Society of Greenbrier
  Valley
(serving SE area)
P.O. Box 1277
Lewisburg, WV 24901-1277
NE area served by Memorial
  Society of Maryland
SW area served by FAMSA
  office

Wisconsin

Funeral Consumer Information
  Society of Greater Milwaukee
13001 W. North Ave.
Brookfield, WI 53005-5214
414-238-0507

Memorial Societies of Wisconsin
6900 Lost Lake Rd.
Egg Harbor, WI 54209-9231
414-868-3136 or 800-374-1109
  (WI only)

Bibliography

DEATH AND DYING

Ariès, Philippe. *The Hour of Our Death*. Trans. by Helen Weaver. New York: Alfred A. Knopf, 1981. (A full-length study by the leading historian of death, expanding on the lectures in the following item.)

———. *Western Attitudes Toward Death: From the Middle Ages to the Present*. Trans. by Patricia M. Ranum. Baltimore and London: Johns Hopkins University Press, 1974. (Classic series of lectures given at Johns Hopkins University on the subject of the shifting attitudes toward death in Western history.)

Dempsey, David. *The Way We Die: An Investigation of Death and Dying in America Today*. New York: Macmillan, 1975. (A well-written series of essays—originally published in the *New York Times Magazine*—on the contemporary death experience, dealing with such issues as euthanasia, violent death, burial procedures, the impact of death on the survivors, and how to have "a natural death.")

Derrida, Jacques. *Aporias*. Trans. by Thomas Dutoit. Palo Alto, Calif.: Stanford University Press, 1993. (A noted French philosopher's thoughts on the meaning of death and dying.)

Doss, Richard W. *The Last Enemy: A Christian Understanding of Death*. New York, Evanston, San Francisco, and London: Harper & Row, 1974. (Written by a Baptist minister for "the serious layman and practicing minister" to deal with questions of death and dying.)

Easson, William M. *The Dying Child: The Management of the Child or Adolescent Who Is Dying.* 2d ed. Springfield, Ill.: Charles C. Thomas, 1981. (A psychiatrist's analysis of the effect of dying on children of various ages, from preschool to adolescent; with chapters on the effect of the child's death on the family and the "treating personnel" as well.)

Fulton, Robert. *Death and Identity.* New York, London, and Sydney: John Wiley & Sons, 1965. (A collection of essays about the sociology and psychology of death; included is Octavio Paz's seminal description of the Mexican folk ceremony the Day of the Dead. Extensive bibliography on psychological and sociological studies of death.)

Furman, Joan, and David McNabb. *The Dying Time: Practical Wisdom for the Dying and Their Caregivers.* New York: Bell Tower, 1997. (A handbook for the dying and their families and friends.)

Gervais, Karen Grandstand. *Redefining Death.* New Haven and London: Harvard University Press, 1986. (An "exploration of the philosophical, medical, and legal definitions of death and of their public policy implications," with bibliography citing academic, legal, and medical sources.)

Graham, Billy. *Facing Death and the Life After.* Minneapolis: Grason, 1987. (The well-known Baptist evangelist's views on the subject.)

Kamath, M. V. *Philosophy of Death and Dying.* Honesdale, Penn.: Himalayan International Institute of Yoga Science and Philosophy, 1978. (Extensive commentaries on death from Eastern and Western religious traditions, including Hinduism, Buddhism, Judaism, Christianity, and Islam, with good bibliography and section on the deaths of famous individuals, ranging from Lord Krishna to Adolf Hitler.)

Kübler-Ross, Elisabeth. *On Death and Dying.* New York: Macmillan, 1969. (The classic study by one of the world's best-known thanatologists, outlining her five stages of the death and grieving process: denial, anger, bargaining, depression, and acceptance.)

———, ed. and intro. *Death: The Final Stage of Growth.* Englewood Cliffs, N.J.: Prentice-Hall, 1975. (A collection of essays elaborating the concept of acceptance of one's own death or that of others as a natural and meaningful last phase of the experience of living. Good chapters on Jewish, Hindu, Buddhist, and Alaskan Inuit death attitudes.)

Kutscher, Austin H. and Lillian G. *Religion and Bereavement: Counsel for the Physician, Advice for the Bereaved, Thoughts for the Clergyman.* New York: Health Sciences Publishing Corp., 1972. (Focus is on Christian—mostly Protestant—and Jewish religions exclusively. Brief list of quotes at end, and an extensive list of classical music selections.)

Levine, Stephen. *A Year to Live: How to Live This Year as If It Were Your Last.* New York: Bell Tower, 1997. (Life changes after confronting the possibility of one's own mortality.)

Mack, Arian, ed. *Death in American Experience.* New York: Schocken, 1973. (Essays on the psychological, sociological, anthropological, and spiritual aspects of death, including an essay on death as a theme in poetry by critic Harold Bloom.)

Metzger, Arnold. *Freedom and Death.* Trans. by Ralph Manheim. London: Human Context Books, 1973. (Theoretical considerations of death, from Plato through Kant and others, stressing its relationship to the philosophical concepts of freedom and free will.)

Meyer, Charles. *Surviving Death: A Practical Guide to Caring for the Dying and Bereaved.* Mystic, Conn.: Twenty-Third Publications, 1988. (Advice for pastors and laypersons especially focused on the needs of caregivers after death. Meyer is an Episcopal priest.)

Neale, Robert E. *The Art of Dying.* New York, Hagerstown, San Francisco, and London: Harper and Row, 1973. (An exercise workbook for dealing with grief; parts appeared in the journal *Pastoral Psychology.*)

Nuland, Sherwin B. *How We Die: Reflections on Life's Final Chapter.* New York: Alfred A. Knopf, 1994. (A professor of the history of medicine at Yale University describes in vivid detail the physical process of dying, including chapters on the five leading causes of death: heart attack, cancer, stroke, Alzheimer's disease, and AIDS.)

Prochnik, Leon. *Endings: Death, Glorious and Otherwise, As Faced by Ten Outstanding Figures of Our Time.* New York: Crown, 1980. (How Sigmund Freud,

Harry Houdini, Isadora Duncan, Zelda Fitzgerald, Yukio Mishima, Dylan Thomas, Malcolm X, and a few more met their ends.)

Saroyan, William. *Obituaries.* Berkeley, Calif.: Creative Arts, 1979. (A book of inspired ramblings by a sixty-eight-year-old playwright on the listing in the annual entertainment newspaper *Variety* of writers and entertainment figures who died during the year 1976.)

Sulzberger, Cyrus. *My Brother Death.* New York: Harper & Brothers, 1961. (Literary and literate reflections on death by a longtime foreign correspondent and columnist of the *New York Times.*)

Wolff, Richard. *The Last Enemy.* Washington, D.C.: Canon Press, 1974. (A thoughtful study of the implications of various Eastern and Western death and funeral traditions by a self-described German Hebrew Christian.)

FUNERAL CUSTOMS AND
THE FUNERAL TRADE

Barley, Nigel. *Grave Matters: A Lively History of Death Around the World.* New York: Henry Holt & Co., 1997. (Though Barley toned down the original British title—*Dancing on the Grave*—the general irreverence of his approach continues in this zippy survey of funeral customs around the world.)

Bennett, Amanda, and Terence B. Foley. *In Memoriam: A Practical Guide to Planning a Memorial Service.* New York: Fireside, 1997. (Includes selection of poetry readings, musical choices, and Christian scriptures.)

Carlson, Lisa. *Caring for Your Own Dead.* Hinesburg, Vt.: Upper Access Publishers, 1987. (The do-it-yourself standard reference book, now in a new edition: *Caring for the Dead: Your Final Act of Love,* 1998.)

Goldman, Rabbi Arnold M. *A Plain Pine Box: A Return to Simple Jewish Funerals and Eternal Traditions.* Hoboken, N.J.: KTAV Publishing House, 1981. (Restoring Jewish funerals to their traditional base.)

Gorer, Geoffrey. *Death, Grief, and Mourning.* New York: Arno Press, 1977. (Orig. ed.: Garden City, N.Y.: Doubleday & Co., 1965.) (Major chronicle of the deterioration of grief and mourning in contemporary Western society, by a British social psychologist.)

Habenstein, Robert W., and William W. Lamers. *Funeral Customs the World Over*. Milwaukee: Bulfin Printers, 1960. (Though the book starts out with an interesting compendium of "funeral customs the world over," covering such outposts as Laos, Mongolia, Bali, and Iran, the appendix gives away the real sponsors of the project: The National Funeral Directors Association of the United States, whose members are listed state by state. Largely follows the professional mortician party line on embalming and other issues.)

Iserson, Kenneth V. *Death to Dust: What Happens to Dead Bodies*. Tucson: Galen Press, 1994. (More than 700 pages of medical and physical details.)

Jones, Constance. *R.I.P.: The Complete Book of Death and Dying*. New York: HarperCollins, 1997. (An encyclopedia or world almanac approach, full of snippets of information about death customs, death science, death culture, death statistics, and how to do funeral arrangements.)

Kalish, Richard A., ed. *Death and Dying: Views from Many Cultures*. Farmingdale, N.Y.: Baywood, 1980. (Explores funeral customs in a number of cultures: Finnish, Mexican, Black American, Appalachian; final section focuses on deaths in wars or disasters, such as plane crashes.)

Lattimore, Richard. *Themes in Greek and Latin Epitaphs*. Urbana: University of Illinois Press, 1962. (A leading translator's expansion on his doctoral thesis on Greek and Roman epitaphs and Greek attitudes toward death, the underworld, and immortality.)

Lynch, Thomas. *The Undertaking: Life Studies from the Dismal Trade*. New York and London: W. W. Norton & Company, 1997. (Witty description and defense of the funeral trade by a small-town Michigan undertaker.)

Mitford, Jessica. *The American Way of Death*. New York: Simon & Schuster, 1963. (The classic attack on the U.S. funeral industry by a tart-tongued British emigrée who deemed herself the last of the great muckrakers.)

——. *The American Way of Death Revisited*. New York: Alfred A. Knopf, 1998. (The state of things twenty-five years later.)

Morgan, Ernest. *Dealing Creatively with Death: A Manual of Death Education and Simple Burial*. 14th ed. Zinn Publications, 1999. (Includes instructions on how to construct a plain pine box coffin.)

O Súilleabháin, Seán. *Irish Wake Amusements*. Trans. by the author from the original Irish. Cork, Ireland: Mercier Press, 1967. (Fascinating account of the history of Irish wakes, detailing the many types of sports and entertainments involved.)

Polen, D. Allen. *The Funeral Arrangement Choice Guide: Helping You Cope with a Loved One's Death*. Ann Arbor, Mich.: Servant Publications, 1996. (Fill-in-the-blank workbook approach.)

Sloane, David Charles. *The Last Great Necessity: Cemeteries in American History*. Baltimore and London: Johns Hopkins University Press, 1991. (A history of graveyards in the United States, from the rural cemetery movement to the contemporary "cemetery in crisis.")

Sublette, Kathleen, and Martin Flagg. *Final Celebrations: A Guide for Personal and Family Funeral Planning*. Ventura, Calif.: Pathfinder Publishing, 1992. (Contains personal stories and a sample general price list for funeral costs.)

Tegg, William. *The Last Act: Being the Funeral Rites of Nations and Individuals*. Detroit: Gale Research Co., 1973. (Original ed.: London: William Tegg & Co., 1976.) (One of the standard surveys of funeral customs from around the world.)

PROSE AND POETRY ANTHOLOGIES

Curtiss, Mina. *Olive, Cypress and Palm: An Anthology of Love and Death*. New York: Harcourt, Brace & Co., n.d. (foreword dated Oct. 13, 1929). (Standard British and American death-related poetry collection.)

Enright, D. J., ed. and comp. *The Oxford Book of Death*. New York and Oxford: Oxford University Press, 1983. (A thorough and literate compendium on various aspects of death.)

Gregory, Horace, ed. and intro. *The Triumph of Life: Poems of Consolation for the English-Speaking World*. New York: Viking, 1943. (Good standard selection, almost exclusively British and American.)

Grierson, Herbert J. C. *Metaphysical Lyrics and Poems of the Seventeenth Century: Donne to Butler*. New York: Oxford/Galaxy, 1959. (A particularly fertile era for inspirational poetry.)

Hadas, Rachel, ed. *Unending Dialogue: Voices from an AIDS Poetry Workshop*. Boston and London: Faber & Faber, 1991. (Fifty-seven poems by ten men with AIDS, part of a poetry workshop held by the Gay Men's Health Crisis in New York City.)

Harris, Jill Werman, ed. *Remembrances and Celebrations: A Book of Eulogies, Elegies, Letters of Condolence, and Epitaphs*. New York: Pantheon, 1999. Eulogies include Winston Churchill on Rupert Brooke, Jordan's King Hussein on Israel's Yitzhak Rabin, and Samuel Carlyle on Ralph Waldo Emerson.

Hoffmann, Yoel, comp. and ed. *Japanese Death Poems: Written by Zen Monks and Haiku Poets on the Verge of Death*. Rutland, Vt., and Tokyo: Charles E. Tuttle Co., 1986. (Powerful short works on the nearness of death.)

Kennedy, Charles W., trans. *An Anthology of Old English Poetry*. New York: Oxford University Press, 1960. (Includes *Beowulf*, "Dream of the Rood," "The Phoenix," and many more appropriate memorializing works.)

Lamont, Corliss. *Man Answers Death: An Anthology of Poetry*. New York: G. P. Putnam's Sons, 1936. (Good selection; an early attempt to include works from cultures other than British and American.)

Mitchell, Stephen, ed. *The Enlightened Heart: An Anthology of Sacred Poetry*. New York: HarperCollins, 1989. (In this and its 1991 companion volume, *The Enlightened Mind: An Anthology of Sacred Prose*, Mitchell makes a heart *vs.* mind distinction between what is "sacred poetry" and "sacred prose." His selections and translations are first rate.)

Ripley, Sherman, ed. *Beyond: An Anthology of Immortality*. New York: D. Appleton & Co., 1930. (A first-rate if somewhat dated collection; poetry only.)

Spiegel, Maura, and Richard Tristman, eds. *The Grim Reader: Writings on Death, Dying, and Living On*. New York: Doubleday Anchor, 1997. (Splendid selection of poetry, prose, and drama on all aspects of dying.)

Theroux, Phyllis, ed. *The Book of Eulogies: A Collection of Memorial Tributes, Poetry, Essays, and Letters of Condolence*. New York: Scribner, 1997. (Recent collection that should set the standard for years to come.)

Untermayer, Louis, ed. *Modern American Poetry*. New York and Burlingame: Harcourt, Brace & World, 1958. (The authoritative American poetry collection for its time, in a new edition.)

———. *Modern British Poetry*. New York and Burlingame: Harcourt, Brace & World, 1958. (The authoritative British poetry collection for the modern era, in a new edition.)

Washington, Peter, ed. *Poems of Mourning*. New York and Toronto: Everyman/Alfred A. Knopf, 1998. (An excellent new anthology, the first substantive one in several years on the subject, including classic and international selections as well as modern works.)

SCRIPTURAL OR SACRED TEXTS AND ANTHOLOGIES

'Alî, 'Abdullah Yûsuf. *The Meaning of the Holy Qur'ân*. Various editions, including Beltsville, Md.: Amana Publications, 1989.

Ballou, Robert O., ed. *The Bible of the World*. New York: Viking Press, 1939. (Included are Hindu, Buddhist, Confucianist, Taoist, Zoroastrian, Judeo-Christian, and "Mohammedan" scriptures. A pocket-sized adaptation, entitled *The Viking Portable Library World Bible*, was issued in 1944.)

Bhagavad Gita, The. Many translations and editions of this Hindu classic, including Eknath Easwaran (Petaluma, Calif.: Nilgiri Press, 1985); Barbara Stoler Miller (New York: Bantam, 1986); and Swami Prabhavananda and Christopher Isherwood (New York: Mentor/New American Library, 1944).

Bierhorst, John, ed. *Four Masterpieces of American Indian Literature: Quetzalcoatl, The Ritual of Condolence, Cuceb, The Night Chant*. Tucson: University of Arizona Press, 1974.

Blackman, Sushila, comp. and ed. *Graceful Exits: How Great Beings Die. Death Stories of Tibetan, Hindu & Zen Masters*. New York and Tokyo: Weatherhill, 1997. (Last words and final descriptions of the passings of enlightened Eastern masters.)

Browne, Lewis, comp. and intro. *The World's Great Scriptures: An Anthology of the Sacred Books of the Ten Principal Religions*. New York: Macmillan Co., 1946. (The ten religions are Christianity, Judaism, Islam, Zoroastrianism, Taoism, Confucianism, Buddhism, Hinduism, and the ancient religions of Babylonia and Egypt.)

Comper, Frances M. M. *The Book of the Craft of Dying and Other Early English Tracts Concerning Death Taken from Manuscripts and Printed Books in the British Museum and Bodleian Libraries*. London: Longmans, Green, & Co., 1917. (A famous anonymous medieval text, *The Book of the Craft of Dying*, plus similar works by William Caxton, Henry Suso, and Richard Rolle, maintaining the original syntax but in modernized spelling.)

Dhammapada, The. Eknath Easwaran, trans. Petaluma, Calif.: Nilgiri, 1986. (A standard Buddhist text.)

Griffiths, Bede, ed. and intro. *Universal Wisdom: A Journey through the Sacred Wisdom of the World*. New York: HarperCollins, 1994. (A selection by a Christian monk who was also a Hindu adept, one of the great proponents of East-West religious dialogue.)

M. *The Gospel of Sri Ramakrishna*. New York: Ramakrishna-Vivekananda Center, 1942. (Words and stories of the great Hindu teacher, 1836–86, whose followers established the Ramakrishna Order.)

Müller, F. Max. *Sacred Books of the East*. 49 vol. plus index. Oxford: Oxford Clarendon Press, 1878–1910. (Still one of the great compendiums of modern religious scholarship, including texts from Hinduism, Buddhism, Jainism, Confucianism, Taoism, Zoroastrianism, and Islam.)

Muslim Prayers. New York: Islamic Center of New York, 1983.

Padwick, Constance. *Muslim Devotions: A Study of Prayer-Manuals in Common Use*. London: S.P.C.K., 1961. (Collection and commentary of prayers of Islam.)

Perry, Whitall N., ed. *A Treasury of Traditional Wisdom*. New York: Simon and Schuster, 1967. (Massive 1,110-page compendium of wisdom writings from all the world's spiritual traditions.)

Pickthall, Marmaduke, trans. *The Meaning of the Glorious Koran.* With an introduction by William Montgomery Watt. New York and Toronto: Alfred A. Knopf/Everyman's Library, 1930 (new ed., 1992). (Generally considered one of the best English versions, along with that by Yûsuf 'Ali.)

Shankaracharya. *Self-Knowledge (Atmabôdha).* Swami Nikhilananda, trans. New York: Ramakrishna-Vivekananda Center, 1974.

Turnbull, Grace H., comp. *Tongues of Fire: A Bible of Sacred Scriptures of the Non-Christian World.* Baltimore: The Johns Hopkins Press, 1941. (Contains Egyptian, Hindu, Jewish, Zoroastrian, Confucian, Taoist, Buddhist, Greek, Roman, and Islamic texts.)

Upanishads, The. Swami Nikhilananda, trans. 4 vol. New York: Ramakrishna-Vivekananda Center, 1949. (Katha Upanishad is in Vol. 1; Chhandogya is in Vol. 4. See also the translation by Shree Purohit Swami and W. B. Yeats, *The Ten Principal Upanishads.* New York: Macmillan Co., 1937.)

Discography

As stated in the chapter on choosing music for the service, these suggestions reflect the taste of the author: a preference for women singers over men; vocal music over instrumental; Beethoven over Mozart; Wagner over Verdi; a special love of folk, country, gospel, and blues; and a distinct dislike of Frank Sinatra (you're on your own finding "My Way"), rap music, heavy metal, and hard-core jazz. Every attempt has been made to make sure that the record labels listed for the songs and other selections are current, but many of these albums are out of print, and the songs—or in some cases whole albums—may have been reissued in a different format or even under a different label: Marian Anderson's classic, **Spirituals**, for example, originally on RCA Victor, has been reissued by a company with the unlikely name (given the subject matter) of Flapper. At any rate, make sure the selection you want is actually on an album, tape, or CD before purchasing it. The list is arranged thematically, not alphabetically.

REQUIEMS AND MEMORIAL SERVICES

A Time of Healing: Music from the Oklahoma City Memorial Service (Warner Bros.): This is an exemplary collection, assembled for the April 23, 1995, ceremony for the 168 persons killed in the bombing of the federal building in Oklahoma City four days earlier. Opening with the stately processional music of the second movement of Beethoven's Seventh Symphony, followed by the soothing strains of the Air from Bach's Suite No. 3, the program also includes (among others) Ravel's touching "Pavane for a Dead Princess"; J. S. Bach's "Bist du Bei Mir" (the tender song he wrote for his wife, Anna Magdalena), hauntingly sung by the Children's Choral Society of Oklahoma; an astonishing instrumental version of "Amazing Grace" arranged by violinist Mark O'Connor; and a stirring finale in which soprano Ernestine Dillard delivers Irving Berlin's "God Bless America" in the best Kate Smith tradition.

Service for Princess Diana (BBC): These are highlights from what was the most watched funeral of all time: that of Diana, Princess of Wales. In addition to readings and personal tributes, the album features the music that was included in the service, including "Libera me" from Verdi's *Requiem;* John Tavener's "Alleluia"; the Anglican hymns "Guide Me, O Thou Great Redeemer" and "Make Me a Channel of Your Peace"; and Elton John's reworking of his song "Candle in the Wind."

Mozart, Requiem: Peter Schreier with the Dresden State Orchestra and the Leipzig Radio Chorus (Philips). Mozart's famous requiem is very formal and a bit bombastic; somewhat quieter sections include "Tuba mirum," "Lacrimosa," and "Benedictus."

Fauré, Requiem: Conducted by Nadia Boulanger (EMI). This beautiful rendering of one of the less stuffy requiems in the classical music repertory is expertly shepherded by the legendary French piano teacher and pioneer woman conductor. The "Sanctus," "Libera me," and "In Paradisum" are all exceptional choices for a service.

Verdi, Requiem Mass: Herbert von Karajan with the Vienna Philharmonic Orchestra (Deutsche Grammophon). Like most Verdi, this mass is full of glorious bombast and full-out choral singing; the highlight remains the hushed rapture of Anna Tomowa-Sintow's solo, "Libera me," which could hold its own at any memorial service.

Brahms, German Requiem: André Previn, with the Royal Philharmonic Orchestra (Teldec). Rather than basing his requiem mass on the Roman Catholic mass of the dead in Latin, like most requiem masses, Brahms takes his texts from various biblical references to death and mourning. There is glorious singing by Margaret Price and Samuel Ramey, along with the

Ambrosian Singers. Another version features Herbert von Karajan and the Vienna Philharmonic (Deutsche Grammophon).

Britten, War Requiem: Benjamin Britten with the London Symphony Orchestra (Decca). The composer starkly contrasts the Latin requiem of the dead with poems by Wilfred Owen, a British poet killed in World War I. The tenor and baritone solos for Peter Pears and Dietrich Fischer-Dieskau are powerful.

George Crumb, Black Angels: Thirteen Images from the Dark Land: Kronos Quartet (Elektra Nonesuch). Composer Crumb's reaction to the Vietnam War is "an arsenal of sounds including shouting, chanting, whispering, gongs, maracas, and crystal glasses." Disturbing sounds for disturbing times—and perhaps not appropriate for more conservative memorial services (though the sections "Pavana Lachrymae" and "Sarabanda da la Muerte Oscura" are beautiful). The same CD contains a forty-part sixteenth-century motet, "Spem in Alium" (Sing and Glorify) by Thomas Tallis; the extraordinary "Doom. A Sigh" by Hungarian composer Istvan Marta (employing actual keening by a woman mourning her dead parents); and Dmitri Shostakovich's Quartet No. 8, dedicated "to the victims of fascism and war."

John Corigliano, Symphony No. 1: Daniel Barenboim and the Chicago Symphony Orchestra (Erato). This American composer's work is dedicated to friends and fellow musicians who have died from AIDS; its tone and structure reflect the anger and heartbreak of those confronting death at an early age. There are moments of great tenderness and lyricism (especially in the third section "Chaconne: Giulio's Song," for two cellos). Perhaps the section most appropriate for a memorial service would be the short epilogue, a hushed juxaposition of various lyric themes by the orchestra, the cellos, and a tinkling offstage piano, so that the symphony ends with a soft whisper.

The AIDS Quilt Songbook: Various composers (Harmonia Mundi). When classical baritone William Parker learned he had the AIDS virus, he refused to give up performing. Quite the contrary, he began commissioning songs for a concert and an album that came to be known as "The AIDS Quilt Songbook." Some of the composers had AIDS themselves; some took texts from poetry by people with AIDS; all had lost friends to AIDS. Highlights include Donald Wheelock's "Fury," Chris DeBlasio's "Walt Whitman in

1989," Ned Rorem's "A Dream of Nightingales," and Annea Lockwood's "For Richard."

CLASSICAL: VOCAL

Maria Callas, Various Collections (EMI): No singer in recorded history has captured the soul of opera like the legendary Maria Callas. Her canon has been well preserved on record, including the following, all from great dramatic roles with which she is identified, and all moments of special tenderness and deep emotional catharsis: "J'ai perdu mon Eurydice," from Gluck's *Orphée and Eurydice;* "Vissi d'arte," from Puccini's *Tosca;* "Casta Diva," from Bellini's *Norma;* and "Mon coeur s'ouvre à ta voix," from *Samson et Dalila,* all from **The Incomparable Callas;** also "Un bel dì vedremo," from *Madama Butterfly;* "Sì. Mi chiamano Mimì," from *La Bohème;* "O mio babino caro," from *Gianni Schicchi;* and "In questa reggia," from *Turandot,* all from **Puccini & Bellini Arias;** and "Adieu, notre petite table," from Massenet's *Manon,* and "Je veux vivre dans ce rêve," from Gounod's *Roméo et Juliette,* both from **Callas à Paris.** For "Sempre libera," from Verdi's *La Traviata,* you have to go to **Maria Callas: Recital** (Movimento Musica).

Jessye Norman, Various Collections: The other great soprano of our age, Norman has mostly recorded a repertory very different from that of Callas, specializing in German opera and vocal music as well as American sacred music. Among her collections are **Scenes from Wagner** (EMI), which includes the "Liebestod" from *Tristan und Isolde,* Brunnhilde's immolation scene from *Götterdämmerung,* the spinning wheel ballad from *Der fliegende Holländer,* and Elsabeth's prayer from *Tannhäuser;* **Strauss Lieder** (Philips), including "Malven," the song Strauss wrote even after his "Four Last Songs" (see below), and such service-appropriate selections as "Ständchen" (Serenade), "Kling!" (Ring!), "Allerseelen" (All Souls' Day), "Lob des Leidens" (In Praise of Sorrow), "Befreit" (Released), and "Traum durch die Dämmerung" (Dream by Twilight); **Sacred Songs** (Philips), with Gounod's "Sanctus" and "O Divine Redeemer," Schubert's "Ave Maria," Franck's "Panis Angelicus," as well as the hymn "Amazing Grace" and the spiritual "Let Us Break Bread Together"; and **At Notre-Dame** (Philips), including the "Et exsultavit" from Bach's *Magnificat,* Bizet's "Agnus Dei," and the spiritual "Go Tell It on the Mountain."

Richard Strauss, Four Last Songs: These sweetly melancholic reflections were written by the German composer shortly before his death. Various sopranos have recorded them, including Kiri Te Kanawa (CBS Masterworks), Lucia Popp (HMV), and Jessye Norman (Philips).

Gustav Mahler, Kindertotenlieder: Mahler wrote these tender and moving "Songs on the Death of Children" after the death of his eldest daughter. Good versions include Christa Ludwig with Herbert von Karajan and the Berlin Philharmonic (Deutsche Grammophon); and Kirsten Flagstad with Sir Adrian Boult and the Vienna Philharmonic. There's also wonderful material in two of Mahler's other song cycles: **Lieder eines fahrenden Gesellen** (Songs of a Wayfarer), recorded by Flagstad (above), as well as by Yvonne Minton, with Sir Georg Solti and the Chicago Symphony (Decca), Dame Janet Baker with pianist Geoffrey Parsons (Hyperion), and Frederica von Stade with Andrew Davis and the London Philharmonic (CBS Masterworks); and **Das Lied von der Erde** (Song of the Earth), by Baker and James King (Philips), Ludwig and René Kollo (Deutsche Grammophon), Minton and Kollo (Decca), and Norman and Jon Vickers (Philips). The strong sense of pastoral calm and beautiful juxtaposition of orchestral texture and vocal line in all these songs make them good selections for a service.

Richard Wagner, Wesendonck Lieder: Besides his operas, Wagner wrote this haunting song cycle celebrating a doomed love affair; its whole mood and ravishing lyric line closely match *Tristan und Isolde,* which he was composing at the same time. Take your pick: the legendary Astrid Varnay (Deutsche Grammophon), Flagstad (London), or Norman (Philips).

Richard Wagner, Operatic Selections: Many, many choices here, including tenor Reiner Goldberg (Capriccio) doing the competition prize song from *Die Meistersinger von Nürnberg,* Tannhäuser's description of his transforming journey to Rome, or Siegmund's power-packed love song "Winterstürme," from *Die Walküre.* Another contemporary tenor, Peter Hoffmann (CBS Masterworks), does the same selections, as well as "Fanget an!" (Begin!), another competition song from *Meistersinger,* and "In fernem Land," the Holy Grail legend from *Lohengrin.*

José Carreras, Placido Domingo, and Luciano Pavarotti, The Three Tenors in Concert (London): Grand opera's other men-of-the-moment deliver pop-opera favorites. Note especially Carreras's "Granada," Pavarotti's "Nessun dorma" (from Puccini's *Turandot*), and Domingo's "O paradis." Then the three combine forces on everything from "Memory" from *Cats* to "Cielito lindo" and "O sole mio."

Andrea Bocelli, Aria: The Opera Album (Philips). The blind pop singer from Italy delivers favorite arias from Puccini, Verdi, and other composers in his high melodic tenor. Highlights that might be good for a service are "Che gelida manina," from Puccini's *La Bohème*; Pinkerton's farewell to Butterfly from *Madama Butterfly*; and the Italian street singer's aria from Strauss's *Rosenkavalier*. Two selections from his other albums are also standouts: "Panis Angelicus" (**Andrea Bocelli**, Universal) and "Time to Say Goodbye," in Italian and English, with British singer Sarah Brightman (**Romanza**, Polydor). This last, so perfect for a memorial service, is listed as "a tribute to Henri Maske." Boccelli and mezzo-soprano Cecilia Bartoli are also featured in **A Hymn for the World** and **A Hymn for the World 2** (both Deutsche Grammophon) with the chorus and orchestra of the National Academy of St. Cecilia in Rome, under conductor Myung-Whun Chung. The albums feature a collection of sacred vocal and choral music written by composers ranging from Bach and Vivaldi to Poulenc and Messiaen.

Georges Bizet, The Pearl Fishers (RCA): The duet "Au fond du temple saint," from *Les Pêcheurs de Perles*, is about as close to heaven as grand opera can get. This version by Jussi Bjoerling and Robert Merrill is on a highlights collection where Bjoerling also sings duets from Puccini and Verdi with sopranos Zinka Milanov, Licia Albanese, and Renata Tebaldi.

George Frideric Handel, Arias for Senesino (Harmonia Mundi): Countertenor Drew Minter sings these uniquely beautiful solos written for the celebrated castrato Senesino by Handel in his operas in the early 1700s.

CLASSICAL: INSTRUMENTAL

Samuel Barber, Adagio for Strings: Arguably the finest and certainly one of the most popular classical works of this century, Barber's Adagio for Strings has the perfect blend of mind and feeling to serve as a memorial touchstone. It calms the soul as it inspires remembrance and reflection. Originally written as the second movement of a string quartet, the work was reshaped by the composer as a separate entity. At around seven minutes it comes in just under the line in terms of length for a service. A perfect opener, it can also close out the program, especially after a particularly thoughtful reading. Various versions are available: Leonard Bernstein's with the Los Angeles Philharmonic (Deutsche Grammophon) is probably the finest, but others by Sir Neville Marriner (Argo), Leopold Stokowski

(HMV), and Eugene Ormandy and the Philadelphia Orchestra (Sony) all probe the resonance of the piece.

Wolfgang Amadeus Mozart, Concerto for Flute and Harp (RCA): Marisa Robles, harp, and James Galway, flute, with the London Symphony Orchestra. This is Mozart in a less heady, more lyrical mood than usual. Most of the composer's works have an icy cleverness that seems too self-contained for memorial services, unless a particular composition was a favorite of the deceased.

Ludwig von Beethoven, Piano Sonatas (Pathétique, Moonlight, Appassionata): The three great sonatas are all too long to be played in their entirety, though a particular movement could be selected for the service. Such solo works should ideally be performed live, but the following records are standard versions of these three, recorded as a set by Vladimir Ashkenazy (Decca), Daniel Barenboim (Deutsche Grammophon), and Alfred Brendel (Philips).

Frédéric Chopin, Piano Sonata No. 2 (RCA): Pianist Emanuel Ax with Eugene Ormandy and the Philadelphia Orchestra. This contains Chopin's famous "Funeral March."

Richard Strauss, Tod und Verklärung (Death and Transfiguration): Though the entire tone poem, at over twenty minutes, is too long for a service, a selection might be excerpted from the first or last sections, editing out the more bombastic blasts. The composer's **Festival Prelude,** for organ and orchestra, is another possible choice for a more formal state or communal affair. (Both are in the set of Strauss's complete tone poems, recorded by Karl Böhm and the Berlin Philharmonic on Deutsche Grammophon).

Johann Sebastian Bach, Goldberg Variations: Pianist Glenn Gould (CBS) explores the soul of Bach.

Arvo Pärt, Tabula Rasa (ECM): These are haunting, understated works by a significant Eastern European minimalist composer. Listen especially to "Cantus in Memory of Benjamin Britten," a memorial of great sweep and power, and the second version of "Fratres," played by twelve cellists of the Berlin Philharmonic.

Henryk Górecki, Symphony No. 3 (Elektra Nonesuch): The contemporary Polish composer subtitled this work a "Symphony of Sorrowful Songs." It is a work of mourning and resolution, slow, subtle, and powerful, employing folk and liturgical forms; parts could be excerpted for a service.

Samuel Barber, Violin Concerto (London): Violinist Joshua Bell gives special care to the slow andante section. Also included on the CD is **Ernest Bloch's** "Baal Shem," with sections entitled "Vidui," referring to the Jewish ceremony of atonement, and "Simchas Torah," denoting the annual festival following the completion of the reading of the Torah.

Ralph Vaughan Williams, The Lark Ascending (Virgin): A beautiful work for violin and orchestra but a bit long for most services at fifteen minutes plus. This version features Christopher Warren-Green on violin and conducting the London Chamber Orchestra. Also included and quite nice is Vaughan Williams's "Fantasia on 'Greensleeves.'" (The same combination is featured on Sir Adrian Boult's HMV version with the London Philharmonic, which also has the composer's "English Folksongs Suite.")

Hietor Villa-Lobos, Bachianas Brasileiras (EMI): Villa-Lobos composed this set of musical homages to Bach, with a flavor of the popular music of his native Brazil. Soprano Victoria de los Angeles sings the beautiful "No. 5" (which Joan Baez did a version of on her own fifth album, also called *No. 5*).

G. I. Gurdjieff/Thomas de Hartmann, The Music of Gurdjieff/de Hartmann: These short piano pieces of folk melodies, religious hymns, and dervish dances were inspired by the travels of Gurdjieff to various religious communities in the Middle East and Asia, then transcribed by composer de Hartmann under Gurdjieff's instructions. Among the most noteworthy selections are "Song of the Fisherwomen," "Hymn from a Great Temple," "Sacred Reading from the Koran," "Orthodox Midnight Hymn," "Sayyid Song and Dance," "Kurd Melody for Two Flutes," the very melodic "On Leaving for Cannes," and the haunting tribute "For Mr. Gurdjieff's Wife." The standard version is by de Hartmann himself (Triangle Records), though a new set of the complete works is being issued by the German record company Wergo Schallplaten. There is also a more popularized and impressive rendition by jazz pianist Keith Jarrett entitled *Sacred Hymns* (Warner Bros./ECM).

John Williams, Theme from *Schindler's List* (MCA): This powerful music contributed greatly to the impact of Steven Spielberg's Holocaust movie,

Schindler's List. There are two versions of the main theme on the sound-track album, both of appropriate length for a service, as well as the similarly haunting "Remembrances" featuring Israeli violinist Itzhak Perlman.

HYMNS, SPIRITUALS, AND GOSPEL MUSIC

Mahalia Jackson: Director Douglas Sirk knew just who to get to sing at the tearful funeral in his splashy 1950 update of the movie *Imitation of Life.* Mahalia Jackson, long hailed without exaggeration as "the world's greatest gospel singer," could raise the rafters and bring down the house like no other singer before or since—even at a funeral. A massive woman with a voice of exceptional power, she left behind a significant recorded legacy on her death in 1972. Almost anything she sang can be used in a service, whether from her early rough-edged sessions on the Grand Award and Apollo labels or from the more sophisticated stylings and arrangements for Columbia Records (they had "more sweetening, but the same soul," she once said in an interview). Examples of the former include "Dig a Little Deeper," "Just As I Am," "I'm Getting Nearer My Home," and "Go Tell It on the Mountain" on **How I Got Over: The Apollo Sessions, 1946–1954** (West Side); the Columbia sessions **(Gospels, Spiritual, & Hymns, Vol. I and II)** include the inimitable "My God Is Real," "I Found the Answer," and such celebrations of the life beyond as "A City Called Heaven," "(Soon I Will Be Done with the) Trouble of the World," "Great Gettin' Up Morning," and "I'm on My Way (to Canaan Land)." Jackson could do it all: spirituals, gospel shouting, standard hymns such as "Take My Hand, Precious Lord," "The Lord's Prayer," and "How Great Thou Art." Whether her singing is slow and sustained ("His Eye Is on the Sparrow," "If I Can Help Somebody") or rollicking and upbeat ("Keep Your Hand on the Plow," "Jesus Met the Woman at the Well,") it's peerless.

Marian Anderson: What Mahalia Jackson was to gospel, Marian Anderson was to classical and concert music. Her album **Spirituals** (RCA/Flapper) remains a treasure trove of selections: "Deep River," "O What a Beautiful City," "Let Us Break Bread Together on Our Knees," "Go Down, Moses," "Were You There (When They Crucified My Lord?)," "(I've Heard of) A City Called Heaven," "Sometimes I Feel Like a Motherless Child," and "Tramping"—all strong selections for a service.

Jessye Norman and Kathleen Battle, Spirituals (EMI): Two leading sopranos who couldn't be more different from each other physically or vocally team up to sing a collection of spirituals dating back to the days of black slavery in America. A first-rate collection of solos and duets.

Aretha Franklin, One Lord, One Faith, One Baptism (Arista): Recorded at her father's church in Detroit, this album features the great rhythm and blues singer returning to her roots in a collection of gospel songs with her father and sisters, plus Mavis Staples of The Staple Singers and Joe Ligon of The Mighty Clouds of Joy. Aretha and her sisters sing "Jesus Hears Every Prayer," and Aretha duos with Staples on "Oh Happy Day" and "We Need Power." The two are joined by Ligon and the other Franklin sisters for the finale, "Packing Up, Getting Ready to Go."

Odetta, The Essential Odetta (Vanguard): Spirituals from the deep-voiced folk favorite of the 1960s. Included here, and especially appropriate to memorials, are "All the Pretty Little Horses," "He's Got the Whole World in His Hands," "No More Auction Block for Me," "Ain't No Grave Can Hold My Body Down," and "Sometimes I Feel Like a Motherless Child."

Staple Singers, The Best of the Staple Singers (Stax/Vee-Jay): This Chicago-based family gospel group sang a mix of new and traditional gospel songs. Included here are "Uncloudy Day," "Stand by Me," "If I Could Hear My Mother Pray Again," "Respect Yourself," and "Sit Down Servant." From the **Freedom Highway** album (Columbia), there's also "Jacob's Ladder," "The Lord's Prayer," and "Will the Circle Be Unbroken."

Sweet Honey in the Rock. Various Titles (Flying Fish Records): This popular black feminist ensemble still does great gospel and spiritual numbers, such as "Study War No More," "Good News," and "Wade in the Waters," but their forte is modern anthems to freedom and equality, including "Ella's Song" ("We who believe in freedom cannot rest/until it comes"), "Breaths" (based on an African poem by Birago Diop), "Biko" (a memorial to a South African martyr), and "Oh Death."

Tennessee Ernie Ford, Hymns (Capitol): This country music singer ("Sixteen Tons") also did a number of religious albums. This one (the first country album to sell a million copies) contains "The Old Rugged Cross," "Sweet Hour of Prayer," "Just a Little Talk with Jesus (Makes It Right)," "Rock of Ages," "Softly and Tenderly," "Abide With Me," and other standard Protestant hymns.

George Beverly Shea, Tender Moments (Star Song Communications): "How Great Thou Art," "Steal Away," "Ninety and Nine," "Have Thine Own Way, Lord," "Abide with Me," "Blessed Assurance," and "Little Brown Church in the Wildwood" are featured in this collection of favorite hymns by the popular singer who toured with the Rev. Billy Graham.

Elvis Presley, Amazing Grace: His Greatest Sacred Hits (RCA): Included are powerful renditions of "I Believe," "Peace in the Valley," "Take My Hand, Precious Lord," "It Is No Secret (What God Can Do)," "In the Garden," "Nearer My God to Thee," "Why Me, Lord?" "Farther Along," "How Great Thou Art," and others.

Additional gospel resources—including white Southern gospel groups and contemporary Christian performers—with their recording companies, are the following: Abyssinian Baptist Gospel Choir (Columbia/Legacy); Acappella (Word); Debby Boone (Benson); Shirley Caesar (Word); Chuck Wagon Gang (CBS); Andrae Crouch (Arrival); Dixie Hummingbirds (MCA); Amy Grant (A&M); Sandi Patti (Word); Sister Rosetta Tharpe (various labels); Clara Ward (Roulette); and BeBe and CeCe Winans (Capitol).

JAZZ AND BLUES

Preservation Hall Jazz Band and Sweet Emma Barrett (Preservation Hall): This group is the original funeral band; they exhibit (among other styles) the New Orleans tradition of jazz musicians following the hearse on foot through the city streets, musically saluting the casket to its final resting place. Sweet Emma was a mainstay of the group as both lead singer and pianist. Even a stroke in 1967 at the age of seventy didn't slow her down; she kept singing and playing one-handed piano until she died fifteen years later. Classic funeral marches that the band and others played on the way to the cemetery included "St. James Infirmary" and "When the Saints Go Marchin' In."

Della Reese, A Date with Della Reese/The Story of the Blues (West Side): Long before she was the saucy senior spirit on TV's *Touched by an Angel,* Della Reese was a blues belter with the best of them. From this double collection (originally on Jubilee), check out "Happiness Is Just a Thing Called Joe," "Someone to Watch over Me," "Empty Bed Blues," "You've Been a Good Old Wagon" (to add a little humor to the service), "St. James Infirmary," "Stormy Weather," "The Nearness of You," and especially "If I For-get You" and "Good Morning Blues." If you can track down her classic ren-dering of "And That Reminds Me" (**The Della Reese Collection**, Varese Vintage), it'll be well worth your search.

Louis Armstrong, Collection (Columbia): These six volumes of recordings feature the world-renowned jazz trumpeter and vocalist, whose roots were in the jazz, blues, and funeral music of New Orleans.

Eubie Blake, Blues and Spirituals (Biograph): Blake was the ultimate rag-time pianist whose career spanned almost eight decades.

Duke Ellington, His Mother Called Him Bill (RCA): This passionate trib-ute album to Ellington's longtime collaborator, Billy Strayhorn, was recorded in just five days shortly after Strayhorn's death in 1967. Ellington also wrote "Come Sunday," which Mahalia Jackson and others have fea-tured. Some of his jazz tunes, such as "Don't Get Around Much Anymore," "Caravan," "Solitude," "Mood Indigo," and "Isfahan" (from his *Far East Suite*), would fit well in a service.

Billie Holiday, The Quintessential (Columbia): Holiday was a legendary blues and jazz singer who died of a drug overdose at the age of thirty-seven. Among the possible selections are "The Very Thought of You," "Strange Fruit," "Fine and Mellow," "Crazy He Calls Me," "Body and Soul," "Am I Blue," "Good Morning Heartache," the especially apt "Please Don't Talk about Me When I'm Gone," and (of course) the classic that she wrote as well as sang: "God Bless the Child."

Aretha Franklin, Aretha Sings the Blues (Columbia): Primarily a tribute to blues singer Dinah Washington (who also died tragically and much too young), Aretha brings great talent and respect to such meaningful Wash-ington standards as "What a Difference a Day Makes" and "This Bitter Earth."

Nina Simone, Best of Nina Simone (Philips): The smoky, sultry voice and rippling piano playing of this enduring artist always make a powerful dra-matic statement. Among the better choices here are "I Loves You Porgy," "Four Women," "Wild Is the Wind," and "Pirate Jenny," all of which make strong statements of mood and commitment. From her other albums there are "Trouble in Mind" and "Nobody Knows You When You're Down and

Out" (**Pastel Blues**, Philips); "The King of Love Is Dead," "Mr. Bojangles," "I Wish I Knew How (It Would Feel to Be Free)," "I Shall Be Released," and "Suzanne" (**The Essential Nina Simone**, RCA); "(I Told Jesus It Would Be All Right) If He Changed My Name" and "Children Go Where I Send You" (**Nina at the Village Gate**, Colpix); "Black Swan," "Theme from Samson and Delilah," and "Cotton Eyed Joe" (**Nina Simone at Carnegie Hall**, Colpix); and "Forbidden Fruit" and "House of the Rising Sun" (**Best of the Colpix Years**, Roulette).

Tracy Nelson, Doin' It My Way (Adelphia): Nelson is a true singer's singer—a Janis Joplin who refused the lure of fame and opted instead for appearing in small clubs and producing her own records, which resonate with country, soul, gospel, and blues. She led the country rock group Mother Earth (Mercury) for a short while before going solo. Here she does remakes of some of the songs she recorded with the group or on her first Mercury solo album, **Tracy Nelson Country**: "I'll Be Long Gone," "Temptation Took Control (Of Me and I Fell)," and the song with which she'll be forever identified, "Down So Low."

Mavis Staples, Mavis Staples (Volt): This member of the famous Chicago gospel group also did a great self-titled solo album in the late 1960s with superb renditions of "A House Is Not a Home," "Until I Met You," and Sam Cooke's "You Send Me."

Alberta Hunter, The Glory of Alberta Hunter (CBS): This superb blues singer made her comeback at the age of eighty in a New York supper club and played there for ten years. Her soft, breathy style and sense of humor made her an instant favorite. Included here: "Give Me That Old Time Religion," "Sometimes I'm Happy," "The Glory of Love," and her witty response to growing old, "You Can't Tell the Difference after Dark."

Lorraine Ellison, Stay with Me (Warner Bros.): Ellison was a singer's singer, a favorite of such stylists as Janis Joplin and Laura Nyro. This hard-to-find album contains her versions of "Only Your Love," "Try (Just a Little Bit Harder)," "Heart Be Still," and the title cut, "Stay with Me" and "You Don't Know Nothing about Love (Until You've Learned the Meaning of the Blues)."

Carrie Smith, When You're Down and Out (Black and Blue): Blues belter in dynamic renditions of "Trouble in Mind," "Nobody Wants You When

You're Down and Out," and "Confessin' the Blues," plus a rollicking version of W. C. Handy's "Saint Louis Blues."

POP AND ROCK

Barbra Streisand, Just for the Record (Columbia): A look at thirty years of recordings by the woman whose versions of pop and Broadway favorites are almost always impeccable. Choose from a long list that includes her stunning rendition of "Happy Days Are Here Again" (not as a political call to arms but as a lonely love ballad), "Moon River," "Cry Me a River," "When the Sun Comes Out" (lots of river and weather songs), "My Man," "People," "A Good Man Is Hard to Find," "Some of These Days," "Silent Night," "Come Rain or Come Shine," "In the Wee Small Hours of the Morning," "God Bless the Child," "There Won't Be Trumpets," "Evergreen," "The Way We Were," "Papa, Can You Hear Me?" "If I Loved You," and "You'll Never Know." Call her pop, easy listening, middle of the road, Broadway, or whatever, Streisand has been the standard-bearer for her generation; her voice is the one most people remember for most of these songs. Missing (among many more, no doubt) from the collection: "As Time Goes By," "Bewitched (Bothered and Bewildered)," and "Make Believe" from **The Third Album** (Columbia) and "Somewhere" and "Being Alive" from **The Broadway Album** (Columbia).

Linda Ronstadt, What's New (Asylum): The pop rock star ventures into old standards with the Nelson Riddle Orchestra: "Guess I'll Hang My Tears Out to Dry," "Someone to Watch Over Me," "What'll I Do," and "Good-bye."

Carly Simon, Torch (Warner Bros.): The sultry-voiced pop singer delivers torch songs, including Stephen Sondheim's "Not a Day Goes By" and Hoagy Carmichael's ironic and understated "I Get Along Without You Very Well."

Willie Nelson, Stardust (Columbia): Another unlikely pairing brings together this country singer-songwriter and old pop standards, and it works beautifully. His low, resonant voice proves the perfect match for songs such as "Stardust," "Georgia on My Mind," "Blue Skies," "Unchained Melody," "September Song," "Moonlight in Vermont," and "Someone to Watch over Me." (Many of Nelson's own songs are equally apropos, including "Funny

How Time Slips Away," "Hello Walls," and "Crazy," his big hit for Patsy Cline (all on **The Best of Willie Nelson,** United Artists).

Bette Midler, Divine Collection (Atlantic): Three of Midler's songs have become virtual pop anthems and are often included in services: "The Rose" (from the film she starred in of the same name, based loosely on the life and death of Janis Joplin), "Wind beneath My Wings" (from another Midler-starring film, *Beaches,* where a woman's best friend dies of cancer), and the celebratory "Friends," with which Midler often opens her live concerts.

Judy Garland, Judy at Carnegie Hall (Capitol): One of the greatest concert albums ever made, by a performer whose career was cut short by drug, alcohol, and personal problems, but whose haunted voice seems to capture all the fragile emotions she experienced. Here are especially touching versions of "Somewhere over the Rainbow" (with which she has been identified since childhood, after playing Dorothy in *The Wizard of Oz*), "If Love Were All," "Come Rain or Come Shine," "Stormy Weather," and "When You're Smiling."

Edith Piaf, Chansons (Capitol): Songs by artists who died young or tragically after lives of great struggle with emotional ups and downs often contain a powerful punch that can be right for some services. This album contains "Des Histoires" (Tales), "Carmen's Story," "Polichinelle" (Punchinella), and especially the inimitable "Les Amants de Teruel" (The Lovers of Teruel), the haunting theme from the film of the same name about two doomed lovers (there's a trumpet solo in the middle of it that sears the soul). **The Very Best of Edith Piaf** (Capitol) has "Milord," "Le Vieux Piano" (The Old Piano), the especially appropriate "Non, Je Ne Regrette Rien" (No, I Regret Nothing), and Piaf's signature piece, "La Vie en Rose."

From Broadway Musicals: "Tomorrow" (*Annie,* CBS); "If Ever I Would Leave You" (*Camelot,* CBS); "There Won't Be Trumpets" (*Anyone Can Whistle,* CBS); "If I Loved You" and "You'll Never Walk Alone" (*Carousel,* MCA); "Memory" (*Cats,* Geffen); "One" and "What I Did for Love" (*A Chorus Line,* CBS); "Being Alive" (*Company,* CBS); "Don't Cry for Me, Argentina" (*Evita,* MCA); "Try to Remember," "Soon It's Gonna Rain," and "They Were You" (*The Fantasticks,* Polydor); "Tradition" and "To Life" (*Fiddler on the Roof,* RCA); "How Are Things in Glocca Morra?" and "Look to the Rainbow"

(Finian's Rainbow, RCA); "Broadway Baby" and "Losing My Mind" *(Follies*, Capitol); "So In Love" *(Kiss Me Kate*, CBS); "I Am What I Am" *(La Cage aux Folles*, RCA); "I Dreamed a Dream," "Stars," "Do You Hear the People Sing?" "In My Life," "On My Own," "Bring Him Home," and "Empty Chairs at Empty Tables" *(Les Misérables*, Encore); "Send in the Clowns" *(A Little Night Music*, CBS); "The Impossible Dream" *(Man of La Mancha*, MCA); "They Call the Wind Maria" *(Paint Your Wagon*, RCA); "Music of the Night" *(Phantom of the Opera*, Polydor); "Come to My Garden" *(The Secret Garden*, Columbia); "Ice Cream" *(She Loves Me*, Polydor); "Make Believe," "Ol' Man River," "Bill," and "You Are Love" *(Show Boat*, EMI), "Climb Every Mountain" and "Edelweiss" *(Sound of Music*, CBS); "Somewhere" *(West Side Story*, CBS).

Bruce Springsteen, Live 1975–85 (Columbia): Springsteen's canon brims with bittersweet attitudes about staying and going, loving and losing, struggling and surviving in the everyday world: "Independence Day," "Nebraska," Woody Guthrie's "This Land Is Your Land" (which Springsteen identifies as Guthrie's "answer to 'God Bless America'"), "Reason to Believe," "Hungry Heart," "Jersey Girl," "The River," "The Promised Land," "Born to Run," "No Surrender," and "Cadillac Ranch" (some of these are full-speed-ahead rock, very upbeat, belying the deep sentiments they contain). Also check out "Book of Dreams" and "Souls of the Departed" from **Lucky Town** (Columbia), and his Oscar-winning "Streets of Philadelphia" for Jonathan Demme's film about AIDS (***Philadelphia* Soundtrack**, Epic).

Janis Joplin, Pearl (Columbia): This album by the soulful rock star, recorded just before her death from a drug overdose, became even more meaningful under those circumstances. Her wailing vocals on "Cry Baby," "A Woman Left Lonely," "Trust Me," and "Get It While You Can" cut to the heart, as do the mournful Kris Kristofferson song "Me and Bobby McGee" and even the throwaway ditty disguised as a prayer "(Oh Lord, Won't You Buy Me a) Mercedes Benz." From the earlier **I Got Dem Ol' Kozmic Blues Again Mama!** (Columbia), there's also "Little Girl Blue," "Work Me, Lord," "As Good As You've Been to This World," and "Try (Just a Little Bit Harder)." And two classics stand out on **Cheap Thrills** (Columbia), her groundbreaking album with Big Brother and the Holding Company: the old Erma Franklin hit "Piece of My Heart" and a unique rendering of George Gershwin's "Summertime."

More Pop and Rock: Seal, "Prayer for the Living" *(Seal*, ZTT); Elton John, "Candle in the Wind," "Daniel," "I Guess That's Why They Call It the

Blues," "Sad Songs (Say So Much)," "Goodbye Yellow Brick Road," "Funeral for a Friend" (*Greatest Hits, Vol. 1–3*, MCA); Bonnie Raitt, Paul Siebel's "Louise" and Jackson Browne's "My Opening Farewell" (*Road Tested*, Capitol); Patti Smith, "People Have the Power," "The Jackson Song," and "Dream of Life" (*Dream of Life*, Arista); The Beatles, "Let It Be," "While My Guitar Gently Weeps," and "The Long and Winding Road" (*Let It Be*, Capitol), and "Norwegian Wood" and "In My Life" (*Rubber Soul*, Capitol); John Lennon, "Imagine" and "(Just Like) Starting Over" (*The John Lennon Collection*, Capitol); Simon and Garfunkel, "Bridge over Troubled Water" (*Bridge over Troubled Water*, Columbia); Procol Harum, "A Whiter Shade of Pale" and "Shine on Brightly" (*Classics*, A&M); Buffalo Springfield, "For What It's Worth," "Bluebird," "Nowadays Clancy Can't Even Sing," "Expecting to Fly," and "Broken Arrow" (*Retrospective*, Atco); Crosby, Stills, Nash & Young, "(Four Dead in) Ohio" (about Kent State) and "Teach Your Children Well" (*So Far*, Atlantic); Don McLean, "American Pie" (*American Pie*, United Artists); Dion, "Abraham, Martin, and John," a song about the assassinations of Martin Luther King and John Kennedy that also was recorded by a host of other singers, from Mahalia Jackson to Emmylou Harris (*Dion, The Right Stuff*); "We Are the World" (various artists, Mercury).

FOLK AND COUNTRY

Judy Collins, Forever: An Anthology (Elektra): Collins has a rich, low contralto that resonates comfort and nurturing. She's been the earth mother of the folk movement for almost four decades now, and this collection contains many songs especially appropriate for memorial services, led by the healing song she wrote after her son's suicide, "The Fallow Way," focusing on the time after harvest when the fields are left unplowed, to recover for another season. No personal details are included; the images are all of nature, describing "the crystal times, the quiet times . . . when winter draws the valley down/and stills the rivers in their storm." Other songs she's written do contain personal details but also the same sense of poetic vision and melodic reflection: "Born to the Breed" (also dedicated to her son Clark), "Grandaddy," "My Father," "Albatross," "Nothing Lasts Forever," "Since You've Asked," and "Walls (We Are Not Forgotten)." There are also other possible choices among the songs by fellow folk writers she's recorded over the years: Ian Tyson's "Someday Soon," Sandy Denny's "Who Knows Where the Time Goes," the traditional "Maid of Constant Sorrow," Mimi Farina's "Bread and Roses," Richard Farina's "Hard-Lovin' Loser," Joni

Mitchell's "Both Sides Now," Pete Seeger's "Turn, Turn, Turn," Leonard Cohen's "Bird on a Wire" and "Suzanne," as well as Collins's classic interpretation of Stephen Sondheim's "Send in the Clowns" and a particularly affecting rendition of "Amazing Grace."

Joan Baez, The First Ten Years (Vanguard): Whereas Collins's voice is low and warm, that of Joan Baez is high and shimmering, like pure crystal. They are contemporaries and have covered much the same type of material over the years, exploring country, classical, and rock as well as folk. This collection showcases Baez at her very finest, especially on such Bob Dylan compositions as "Farewell Angelina," "Love Is Just a Four-Letter Word," "A Hard Rain's a-Gonna Fall," and "There But for Fortune," by Phil Ochs. Her readings of the old English Childe ballads are unequaled; included here are three such tales of love and death: "John Riley," "Mary Hamilton," and "Geordie." Three other clear possibilities show the range of material that Baez has mined over the years: "Manha de Carnaval," from the movie *Black Orpheus,* a Brazilian carnival setting of the Greek legend of Orpheus going to the underworld to rescue his wife, Eurydice; "No Expectations," a haunting Rolling Stones song about going on with one's life no matter what the obstacles; and "Sweet Sir Galahad," written about her sister Mimi Farina's recovery after her husband Richard's early death. Other potential Baez selections bridge all types of music: gospel in "Let Us Break Bread Together" (a tribute to Marian Anderson) and "Freedom" (**Recently**, Gold Castle); classic country in "Banks of the Ohio," "Long Black Veil," "Will the Circle Be Unbroken," and "I Still Miss Someone" (**The Country Music Album**, Vanguard) and "The Wild Mountain Thyme" and "The River in the Pines" (**The Lovesong Album**, Vanguard); and her own unique mix of country, folk, pop, and rock in Bob Dylan's "Forever Young," John Lennon's "Imagine," and her own "Diamonds and Rust" on **Classics**, A&M, which also contains her version of "Amazing Grace."

Bob Dylan, Biograph (Columbia): Dylan, whose career has undergone several radical shifts over the years—from radical-politics folkie to country crooner to electric-guitar rock, then increasingly into his own personal brand of mysticism—has written an assortment of songs that are especially apt for memorial services. Leading the pack is the much-recorded "I Shall Be Released," first issued on the **Music for Big Pink** album with The Band (Capitol), which also contains such gems as "This Wheel's on Fire," "Long Black Veil," and "Tears of Rage." "I Shall Be Released" is also on this career-spanning retrospective (**Biograph**), as are such choices as "Forever Young,"

"Knockin' on Heaven's Door," "Time Passes Slowly (Up Here in the Mountains)," "Gotta Serve Somebody," the enigmatic and compelling "Mr. Tambourine Man," "Visions of Johanna," "Lay Down Your Weary Tune," and (from the really early days) "Lonesome Death of Hattie Carroll," "Like a Rolling Stone," and "Blowin' in the Wind." Dylan summed up the life stories of more than one generation in his tunes and lyrics, and his songs stand the test of time. One final favorite: the mysterious "Sad Eyed Lady of the Lowlands" (with the line "my warehouse eyes, my Arabian drums, should I put them by your gate, or sad-eyed lady, should I wait?") from **Blonde on Blonde** (Columbia).

Leonard Cohen, The Best of (Columbia): Following close behind Dylan as poet-songwriter of a generation is Canadian Leonard Cohen. His flat but haunting voice is not everyone's cup of tea, but the interpretations he gives his own songs are uniquely powerful. This collection includes most of the best-known favorites: "Suzanne," "Sisters of Mercy," "So Long, Marianne," "Bird on a Wire," "Famous Blue Raincoat," and "Hey, That's No Way to Say Goodbye."

Mary Chapin Carpenter, Shooting Straight in the Dark (Columbia): One of the finest singer-songwriters of the 1990s, mostly known for her upbeat romps "Down at the Twist and Shout," "Shut Up and Kiss Me," and "I Feel Lucky," she's also penned some powerfully reflective, memory-laced ballads, such as "Halley Came to Jackson," "The Moon and St. Christopher," and "Middle Ground" from this major album. But probably the best choice among her songs for a service would be "Why Walk When You Can Fly," from the **Stones in the Road** album (Columbia), which contains these lyrics: "And in this world there's a whole lot of golden / In this world there's a whole lot of plain / In this world you've a soul for a compass / And a heart for a pair of wings. . . . / For the rest of the time that you're given / Why walk when you can fly."

Meredith Monk, Dolmen Music (ECM): Not really a folk or a country singer, Monk is unclassifiable. She nonetheless writes storylike songs for dancelike theater pieces in which she appears. They derive from deep in some mythic past and linger long in the soul. At times, words dissolve completely into sheer sound (as in Strauss's *Daphne,* in which the main character turns slowly into a tree at the end of the opera); at other times, lyrics evoke a childlike state of being that is at the same time otherworldly. She once sang "Gotham Lullaby" at a memorial service, and I've never forgotten it. From this same collection, there's also "Travelling," "The Tale," and her suite *Dolmen Music,* which seems to summon up ancient spirits of mourning, then set them free. On a second collection, **Do You Be** (ECM), there's "Scared Song," "Memory Song," the title song, "Quarry Lullaby," and "Panda Chant I and II."

Various Artists, **Time and Love: The Music of Laura Nyro** (Astor Place): This tribute album to the late singer-composer features renditions of several of her songs that would make good choices for a service: "Time and Love" (Phoebe Snow), "Save the Country" (Roseanne Cash), "Eli's Coming" (Lisa Germano), "Upstairs by a Chinese Lamp" (Leni Stern), and "And When I Die" (Sweet Honey in the Rock). If anyone needs convincing of Nyro's status as a songwriter, this should do it.

Various Artists, **Tammy Wynette Remembered** (Asylum): Another tribute album, to one of the great stars of country music. The songs themselves become memorials, especially "Take Me to Your World," sung by Wynette's one-time husband and singing partner, George Jones; "'Til I Get It Right," by Trisha Yearwood; "Woman to Woman," by Wynonna; "Golden Ring" by Emmylou Harris, Linda Ronstadt, and Kate and Anna McGarrigle; and (especially) "'Til I Can Make It on My Own," by Faith Hill. Forget the mishmash Elton John makes of Wynette's signature piece, "Stand by Your Man," though, and go directly to the source (**Tammy Wynette, Anniversary: Twenty Years of Hits,** Epic), which has the originals for all these cover versions.

Will the Circle Be Unbroken (EMI): Old-time country greats including Mother Maybelle Carter, Earl Scruggs, Doc Watson, Roy Acuff, Merle Travis, Jimmy Martin, and others join the Nitty Gritty Dirt Band in traditional country gospel favorites, among them the title song, "Keep on the Sunny Side," "Precious Jewel," "I Saw the Light," "I Am a Pilgrim," and "Wildwood Flower." For the Carter family itself (A.P., Sara, and Maybelle), their canon is available on RCA and Rounder Records.

Jean Ritchie, Mountain Born (Greenhays): Born to a very musical family (with fourteen children) in the Cumberland Mountain region of Kentucky, Ritchie went on to a successful career as a folksinger in New York City starting in the 1950s. This recent collection shows she's lost none of her skill as a singer and dulcimer player of traditional music. "Abigail" is a tribute to her mother; "When Sorrows Encompass Me Round" and "Our Meeting Is Over" are old Baptist hymns; and "My Dear Companion" is an old family love song that serves as a very appropriate farewell.

Other Folk Music: Ian and Sylvia, the Canadian husband-and-wife duo whose voices blended so perfectly in "Early Morning Rain," "Four Strong Winds," "You Were on My Mind," and "Spanish Is a Loving Tongue" (*Greatest Hits*, Vanguard); Buffy Sainte-Marie, Cree Indian singer-songwriter whose voice has a wild vibrato and whose compositions ricochet from the personal to the political to the spiritual in "God Is Alive, Magic Is Afoot," "Universal Soldier," "Winter Boy," "Until It's Time for You to Go," "Take My Hand for Awhile," and "My Country 'Tis of Thy People You're Dying" (*The Best of*, Vanguard); Jim and Jean, another folk duo, best known for their versions of two Phil Ochs songs, "Changes" and "Crucifixion" (*Changes*, Verve); Joni Mitchell, "I Had a King," "Michael from Mountains," "Song to a Seagull" (*Joni Mitchell*, Reprise) and "Chelsea Morning" and "Both Sides Now" (*Clouds*, Reprise); Pete Seeger, "Turn, Turn, Turn" (adapted from Ecclesiastes, "To every thing there is a season . . ."), "If I Had a Hammer," "We Shall Overcome," "Guantanamera," "Last Night I Had the Strangest Dream" (*The World of Pete Seeger*, Columbia).

Other Country Music: Vince Gill, "Go Rest High on That Mountain," written after his brother's early death (*When Loves Finds You*, MCA); Kenny Chesney, "Grandpa Told Me So" (*All I Need to Know*, BNA); Rick Trevino, "Un Rayo de Luz," about a mother who leaves a light on for her son who's afraid of monsters in the shadows of his room (*Un Rayo de Luz*, Sony Discos); Dolly Parton, Linda Ronstadt, and Emmylou Harris, "My Dear Companion," "Those Memories of You," "Rosewood Casket," and "Farther Along" (*Trio*, Warner Bros.); Loretta Lynn, Dolly Parton, and Tammy Wynette, "Silver Threads and Golden Needles," "Wings of a Dove," "Let Her Fly," and "I Dreamed of a Hillbilly Heaven" (*Honky Tonk Angels*, Columbia); Suzy Boggus, Alison Krauss, and Kathy Mattea, "Teach Your Children Well," Mary Chapin Carpenter, "Willie Short," Johnny Cash, "Forever Young," Wilco, "The TB Is Whipping Me" (all from *Red Hot + Country*, a benefit album by country artists for AIDS research, Mercury); The Byrds, "I Am a Pilgrim," "You Ain't Going Nowhere," and "Nothing Was Delivered" (*Sweetheart of the Rodeo*, Columbia); Pam Tillis, "The River and the Highway" (*All of This Love*, Arista); George Jones, "He Stopped Lovin' Her Today" (*Greatest Hits*, Epic); Joe Diffie, "Prop Me Up Beside the Jukebox (When I Die)" (*Honky Tonk Attitude*, Epic); Marty Robbins, "El Paso" and "Streets of Laredo" (*Essential*, Columbia); Emmylou Harris, "Wayfaring

Stranger," "Green Pastures," "Jordan," "Darkest Hour Is Just Before Dawn" (*Roses in the Snow,* Warner Bros.); Patsy Cline, "I Fall to Pieces," "Heartaches," "Walking after Midnight," "Sweet Dreams" (*The Patsy Cline Story,* MCA).

INTERNATIONAL

Global Divas: Voices from Women of the World (Rounder): This is a unique collection of recordings from women singers from various cultures. Among the legends are not only familiar names such as Marlene Dietrich and Edith Piaf but also Egypt's legendary Oum Kalsoum; Brazil's Gal Costa, Maria Bethania, and Elis Regina; South Africa's Mahotella Queens; Cuba's Celina González and Celia Cruz; Mali's Oumou Sangare; Lebanon's Fairuz; Spanish flamenco singer Carmen Linares; Argentina's Mercedes Sosa; and the Bulgarian State Radio and Television Female Vocal Choir, whose album *Le Mystère des Voix Bulgares* was a surprise runaway hit when released in the United States by Elektra/Nonesuch in 1987. This three-CD sampler set might prove a gold mine if you are looking for exotic fare for the service.

Voices of Forgotten Worlds: Traditional Music of Indigenous People (Ellipsis Arts): This is a collection of traditional music, much of it ceremonial, from around the world: pan pipes from the Solomon Islands, a gamelan orchestra from Bali, a mourning song from aboriginal Taiwan, pygmy music from central Africa, and several Inuit and Native American selections.

Nusrat Fateh Ali Khan, Devotional Songs (Real World): This Pakistani singer was the world's foremost proponent of *qawwali,* or Sufi devotional music. Not used in religious ceremony (where music is not allowed in mainstream Islam), it is intended instead to bring a sense of the sacred into everyday life (usually the domain of secular music). Basically, the songs are all love songs, but as in the poetry of the Persian poet Rumi, the love object is God. The music has a meditative quality but at the same time a constant pulse that can only be described as ecstatic. "Allah Hoo Allah Hoo" from this album is an especially compelling selection.

Ravi Shankar, Farewell, My Friend (EMI India): The great sitar master made this album in homage to his Indian film director friend Satyajit Ray.

Gyuto Monks: Tibetan Tantric Choir (Windham Hill): This religious chanting of Tibetan Buddhist monks, with overtone singing (an extraordinary vocal technique in which a single singer produces two separate notes at the same time) and traditional instruments (conch shells, cymbals, long copper horns, and bone trumpets), creates an extraordinary and hypnotic effect and could be used to great effect in some services.

Gilberto Gil and Jorge Ben, Xango/Ogum (Phonogram): This album by two of the leading singer-composers of Brazil celebrates two gods (Xango, the fire god, and Ogum, the god of iron) of that country's fascinating *candomblé*, with roots back to the Yoruba religion of Nigeria and strong links to Roman Catholicism, the nominal faith of the land. The most extraordinary cut on the album is "Filhos de Gandhi," in which Gil traces a universal lineage from Gandhi to all liberation movements.

King Sunny Ade and His African Beats, Aura (Island): Ade is the leading exemplar of juju music from Nigeria, a glorious, celebratory kind of music that (like *qawwali* or the Brazilian music mentioned above) refuses to acknowledge borders between the spiritual and secular, praising the divine in everyday life. These songs, including "Ase," "Ire," "Oremi," and "Iro," are actually prayers (King Sunny Ade is actually a priest-king among the Yoruba) of tremendous joy and affirmation.

Ladysmith Black Mambamzo, Ulwandle Oluncgwele (Shanachie): This South African a cappella choir, which sings hymns of exceptional harmonic complexity and breathtaking beauty, was popularized by Paul Simon in the late 1980s, but the music has lasting importance.

Robbie Robertson, Contact from the Underworld of Redboy (Capitol): Former mainstay of The Band, Canadian Robbie Robertson has been exploring his own Native roots for the past few years in album and video collaborations with other Native American artists. Particularly affecting selections here include the hypnotic "Peyote Healing," "The Code of Handsome Lake," "Unbound," and "Stomp Dance (Unity)."

Endnotes

1. FIRST STEPS

1. Helen M. Luke, "Suffering," from *Old Age* (New York: Parabola Books, 1987), 103–4, 107.

2. THE STANDARD SOLUTION: USING THE SERVICES OF PROFESSIONALS

1. Interfaith Funeral Information Committee Web site, www.xroads.com, under "Funerals and Ripoffs" section.
2. *The New Grolier Multimedia Encyclopedia*, "Embalming" (On-line Computer Systems, 1993).
3. D. Allen Polen, Jr., *The Funeral Arrangement Choice Guide* (Ann Arbor, Mich.: Servant Publications, 1996), 47.
4. IFIC Web site, under "Protective Seal Caskets."
5. Wilfrid Sheed, quoted on IFIC Web site under "Damage to Religious Rites, Family Customs, Traditions." Sheed was writing in the Catholic publication *Jubilee* in 1960.
6. James Farrell, *Inventing the American Way of Death, 1830–1920* (Philadelphia: Temple University Press, 1980), quoted in Lisa Carlson, *Caring for the Dead: Your Final Act of Love* (Hinesburg, Vt.: Upper Access Press, 1998), 44.
7. Josephine Black Pesaresi, "'Simple and Cheap,' My Father Said," from the newsletter of the Funeral Consumer Information Society of Connecticut, Inc., Newsletter, Winter 1998 (Vol. 1, No. 1); (posted on the Web site of the Funeral and Memorial Services of America, www.funerals.org/famsa.

3. FIRST ALTERNATIVE: CREMATION

1. George Bernard Shaw, "On the Cremation of His Mother," letter to Stella Campbell, Feb. 22, 1913; anthologized in *The Grim Reader: Writings on Death, Dying, and Living On*, ed. Maura Spiegel and Richard Tristman (New York: Doubleday Anchor, 1997), 287.

2. Constance Jones, in *R.I.P.: The Complete Book of Death and Dying* (New York: HarperCollins, 1997), lists a number of other countries that practiced the same custom: China, Thrace, Scythia, Egypt, Africa, Polynesia, and Scandinavia.

3. Richard Selzer, "Remains," from *Letters to a Young Doctor* (Borchardt, 1982), anthologized in *The Grim Reader*, 292.

4. SECOND ALTERNATIVE: PRIVATE SERVICE AND HOME BURIAL

1. Ernest Morgan, *Dealing Creatively with Death: A Manual of Death Education and Simple Burial*, 14th ed. (Zinn, 1999).

2. Steve Carlson, "Mary Jane," in Lisa Carlson, *Caring for the Dead*, 25–26.

6. A BRIEF BACKGROUND OF AMERICAN FUNERAL CUSTOMS

1. Geoffrey Gorer, *Death, Grief, and Mourning* (New York: Doubleday & Co., 1965), xxxii.

2. Ibid., xxxiii.

3. Philippe Ariès, quoted in *The Grim Reader*, 296.

4. Thomas F. Garrity and James Wyss, "Death, Funeral and Bereavement Practices in Appalachian and Non-Appalachian Kentucky," from *Death and Dying: Views from Many Cultures*, ed. Richard A. Kalish (Farmingdale, N.Y.: Baywood, 1980), 104.

5. Ibid., 105.

6. Charles O. Jackson, "Death Shall Have No Dominion: The Passing of the World of the Dead in America," from *Death and Dying*, 47.

7. HISTORICAL AND NON-WESTERN FUNERAL TRADITIONS

1. C. P. Cavafy, "The Horses of Achilles," from *The Collected Poems,* trans. by Edmund Keeley and Philip Sherrard (Princeton, N.J.: Princeton University Press, 1975).

2. William Tegg, *The Last Act: Being the Funeral Rites of Nations and Individuals* (Detroit: Gale Research Co., 1973; original ed., London: William Tegg & Co., 1876), 38–39.

3. Ibid., 35.

4. Rex L. Jones, "Religious Symbolism in Limbu Death-by-Violence," from *Death and Dying,* 29.

5. *The Meaning of the Holy Qur'ân,* translation by 'Abdullah Yûsuf 'Alî (many editions, including Beltsville, Md.: Amana Publications, 1997, 9th ed.), 32:2–4.

6. *Muslim Prayers* (New York: The Islamic Center of New York, 1983), 54.

7. *The Meaning of the Holy Qur'ân,* 20:55.

8. *Muslim Prayers,* 67–68.

9. Seán O Súilleabháin, *Irish Wake Amusements* (Cork, Ireland: Mercier Press, 1967), 11, 26.

10. Ibid., 172.

11. Quotes from Catherine Falk, "Hmong Funeral in Australia in 1992," *Hmong Studies Journal* 1:1 (Fall 1996), on the Internet at www.como.stpaul. k12.mn.us/Vue-Benson/HSJv1n1Falk.html.

12. Here Falk quotes from an unpublished master's thesis by Megan McNamer, "Song of Self: A Study in Identity in Hmong Music," University of Washington, 1986.

13. Here Falk quotes a Vietnamese speaker, Vaj Suav Vaj, from an article by Nicholas Tapp, "Hmong Religion," in *Asian Folklore Studies* 48 (1989), 60. All following quotes about the Hmong from Falk, "Hmong Funeral in Australia 1992."

14. Navajo chant, quoted by Joseph Epes Brown in "Becoming Part of It," from *I Become Part of It* (New York: Parabola Books, 1989), 20.

15. Seyyed Hossein Nasr has described the Sufi concept of *fanâ',* or annihilation, and its relationship to *dhikr* (constant repetition of the name of Allah) as follows: "Sufism uses the quintessential form of prayer, the *dhikr* or invocation, in which all otherness and separation from the Divine is removed and man achieves *tawhîd* [unity]. Though this process of transforming man's psyche appears gradual at first, the *dhikr* finishes by becoming man's real nature and the reality with which he identifies himself. With the help of the *dhikr,* as combined with appropriate forms of meditation or *fikr,* man

first gains an integrated soul, pure and whole like gold, and then in the *dhikr* he offers this soul to God in the supreme form of sacrifice. Finally in annihilation *(fanâ')* and subsistence *(baqâ')* he realizes that he never was separated from God even from the outset." Nasr, *Sufi Essays* (Albany: State University of New York Press, 1991), 49–50.

16. Lao Tsu, *Tao Te Ching,* trans. by Gia-Fu Feng and Jane English (New York: Alfred A. Knopf, 1972), chapter 16.

10. SPECIAL CIRCUMSTANCES

1. Kathleen Sublette and Martin Flagg, *Final Celebrations: A Guide for Personal and Family Funeral Planning* (Ventura, Calif.: Pathfinder Publishing, 1992), 93–94 (summarized from an article by Beverly Godwin in *Thanatos,* Spring 1991).

13. THE RIGHT WORDS: SELECTING POETRY AND PROSE

1. Edith Sitwell, "Eurydice," from *The Collected Poems* (New York: Vanguard, 1968), 263.

2. Wendell Berry, "Testament," from *Collected Poems 1957–1982* (San Francisco: North Point Press, 1984).

3. Michelangelo Buonarotti, "To Luigi del Riccio after the Death of Cecchino Bracci," from *The Sonnets of Michelangelo* (Garden City: Doubleday & Co., 1970), anthologized in *Poems of Mourning,* comp. and ed. by Peter Washington (New York and Toronto: Alfred A. Knopf, 1998), 80.

4. Czeslaw Milosz, "On Parting with My Wife, Janina," from *The Collected Poems 1931–1987* (New York: Viking, 1988), anthologized in *Poems of Mourning,* 107–8.

5. Seamus Heaney, "Clearances, #3," from *Selected Poems 1966–1987* (New York: Farrar Strauss & Giroux, 1990), 248.

6. *Japanese Death Poems: Written by Zen Monks and Haiku Poets on the Verge of Death,* comp. and intro. by Yoel Hoffmann (Rutland, Vt., and Tokyo: Charles C. Tuttle, 1986), 244.

7. Ibid., 248.

8. Ibid., 252.

9. Harlan Hubbard, *Shantyboat on the Bayous* (Lexington: University Press of Kentucky, 1990), 69. Quoted in Wendell Berry, *Harlan Hubbard: Life and Work* (Lexington: University Press of Kentucky, 1990), 74.

10. Ralph Waldo Emerson, "Circles," from *Selections*, ed. by Stephen E. Whicher (Boston: Houghton Mifflin Co., 1957), 177–78.

11. C. S. Lewis, *A Grief Observed* (London: Faber & Faber, 1961), anthologized in *The Oxford Book of Death*, comp. and ed. by D. J. Enright (Oxford and New York: Oxford University Press, 1983), 114.

12. Arthur Waley, *Three Ways of Thought in Ancient China* (London: George Allen & Unwin, 1939), reprinted in *Oxford Book of Death*, 113.

13. Rumi, "The Ascending Soul," from *Rumi: Poet and Mystic*, trans. by Reynold A. Nicholson (London: G. Allen & Unwin, 1950).

14. WRITING EULOGIES

1. *The Book of Eulogies: A Collection of Memorial Tributes, Poetry, Essays, and Letters of Condolence*, edited and with commentary by Phyllis Theroux (New York: Scribner, 1997), 14–15.

2. Susan Gilbert Dickinson, quoted in *Book of Eulogies*, 30.

3. Eugene McCarthy, *Up 'Til Now: A Memoir* (New York: Harcourt Brace & Co., 1987); *Book of Eulogies*, 86.

4. Winston Churchill, *His Complete Speeches, Vol. VI, 1935–1942*, ed. by Robert Rhodes James (New York: Chelsea House, 1974); *Book of Eulogies*, 61.

5. Ralph Waldo Emerson, quoted in *Book of Eulogies*, 93–95.

6. Leon Joseph Cardinal Suenens, quoted in *Book of Eulogies*, 106.

7. Helen Keller, *Midstream: My Later Life* (New York: Doubleday, Doran & Co., 1929); *Book of Eulogies*, 285–86.

8. Kim Stafford, "My Father's Place," *Hungry Mind Review* (Winter 1993–94); *Book of Eulogies*, 47.

9. W. H. Auden, "In Memory of W. B. Yeats," from *Collected Poems*, ed. by Edward Mendelson (New York: Random House, 1940); *Book of Eulogies*, 37.

10. Obituary of Marian Anderson, *New York Times*, Feb. 9, 1993; *Book of Eulogies*, 165.

11. Robert F. Kennedy, speech, April 4, 1968; *Book of Eulogies*, 157.

12. Dr. Martin Luther King, speech in September 1963, "The Martyred Children of Birmingham"; *Book of Eulogies*, 147–48.

13. Mario Cuomo, *More Than Words: The Speeches of Mario Cuomo* (New York: St. Martin's Press, 1993), 296–97 (speech at Pierre Hotel in NYC, March 9, 1993).

15. CHOOSING SPIRITUAL OR
SCRIPTURAL REFERENCES

1. Shankaracharaya, *Atmabôdha (Self-Knowledge)*, trans. by Swami Nikhilananda (New York: Ramakrishna-Vivekananda Center, 1974), verses 31, 32, 34–36; pp. 147–49.

2. Chuang Tzu, cited in Whitall Perry, *A Treasury of Traditional Wisdom* (New York: Simon and Schuster, 1967), 223. From *Les Pères du Systeme taoïst*, trans. by Léon Wieger (Paris: Cathasia, 1950).

3. Farid ud-Din Attar, *The Conference of the Birds*, trans. by C. S. Nott (New York: Samuel Weiser, 1969), 123–24.

4. *Book of the Craft of Dying* (London: Compter's, 1917), cited in *Treasury of Traditional Wisdom*, 215.

5. *The Sacred Pipe: Black Elk's Account of the Seven Rites of the Oglala Sioux*, recorded and edited by Joseph Epes Brown (Norman: University of Oklahoma Press, 1953), 8.

6. *The Upanishads*, trans. by Swami Nikhilananda (New York: Ramakrishna-Vivekananda Center, 1949), vol. 1, pp. 140–41 (Katha Upanishad I.ii.18–20).

7. Dante Alighieri, *Paradiso*, trans. by John Ciardi (New York: New American Library, 1961), 365 (*Paradiso* XXXIII, 145).

8. Karlfried Graf Dürckheim, *The Call for the Master: The Meaning of Spiritual Leadership on the Way to the Self* (New York: E. P. Dutton, 1989), excerpted in *Parabola: The Magazine of Myth and Tradition*, XV, No. 3 (Fall 1990, "Liberation" issue), 10.

9. Frithjof Schuon, *Understanding Islam*, rev. trans. (Bloomington, Ind.: World Wisdom Books, 1994), 92.

10. *The Gospel of Sri Ramakrishna*, trans. by Swami Nikhilananda (New York: Ramakrishna-Vivekananda Center), 88.

11. Chandogya Upanishad, VI.viii.6, cited in *Treasury of Traditional Wisdom*, 225.

12. Kahlil Gibran, *The Prophet* (New York: Alfred A. Knopf, 1923), 81.

13. "The Night Chant," from *Four Masterworks of American Indian Literature*, ed. by John Bierhorst, trans. from the Navajo by Washington Matthews, 328–30.

17. SETTING THE SCENE: FLOWERS,
PHOTOS, PERSONAL MEMENTOS

1. Frithjof Schuon, "Esthétique et symbolisme dans l'art et la nature" ("Aesthetics and Symbolism in Art and Nature"), from *Perspectives spirituelles et faits*

humains (Paris: Éditions Maisonneuve & Larose, 1989), 34–35 (trans. by Rob Baker).

2. In the essay mentioned above, Schuon (who was also an accomplished painter) gives an elaborate analysis of color symbolism and the spiritual effect of various color combinations. See also Martin Lings, "The Symbolism of the Triad of Primary Colors," in *Symbol and Archetype* (Cambridge, Eng.: Quinta Essentia, 1991), 29–44.

18. POST-CELEBRATION ACTIVITIES: FOOD, DRINK, CAMARADERIE

1. Harlan Hubbard letter to Harvey Simmonds, June 19, 1986. Quoted in Berry, *Harlan Hubbard*, 77.

TWO SAMPLE MEMORIAL SERVICES

1. John Donne, "Death Be Not Proud," from *Holy Sonnets* (various editions).
2. "The Phoenix," from *An Anthology of Old English Poetry*, trans. by Charles W. Kennedy (New York: Oxford University Press, 1960), 102–11.
3. Marguerite Yourcenar, *With Open Eyes: Conversations with Matthieu Galey*, trans. by Arthur Goldhammer (Boston: Beacon Press, 1984), 260.
4. William Shakespeare, *The Tempest*, IV.1.148–57 (various editions).
5. *The Meaning of the Holy Qur'ân*, 16:68–70.
6. Ogden Nash, "The Purist," from *I Wouldn't Have Missed It: Selected Poems of Ogden Nash* (Boston: Little Brown & Co., 1975).
7. Norman Maclean, *Young Men and Fire* (Chicago: University of Chicago Press, 1992), 298–301.

About the Author

A native of Indiana and a graduate of Indiana University, Rob Baker was the pop music columnist for *The Chicago Tribune* in the late 1960s. He moved to New York City in 1969 and over the course of the next two decades reviewed music, dance, theater, and film while working as an editor for various publications, including *DanceMagazine, The Soho Weekly News, New York Daily News,* and *Women's Wear Daily.* His books include *Bette Midler: An Unauthorized Biography* and *The Art of AIDS: From Stigma to Conscience.* From 1987 to 1992, he was coeditor of *Parabola: The Magazine of Myth and Tradition.* In 1994, he moved to Lexington, Kentucky, where he works as a freelance writer, editor, and translator.

Other Bell Tower Books

*Books that nourish the soul, illuminate the
mind, and speak directly to the heart*

Valeria Alfeyeva
PILGRIMAGE TO DZHVARI
A Woman's Journey of Spiritual Awakening
An unforgettable introduction to the riches of
the Eastern Orthodox mystical tradition. A modern *Way of a Pilgrim*.
0-517-88389-9 Softcover

Cynthia Bourgeault
LOVE IS STRONGER THAN DEATH
The Mystical Union of Two Souls
Both the story of the incandescent love between two hermits
and a guidebook for those called to this path of soulwork.
0-609-60473-2 Hardcover

Madeline Bruser
THE ART OF PRACTICING
Making Music from the Heart
A classic work on how to practice music which combines
meditative principles with information on body mechanics and medicine.
0-609-80177-5 Softcover

Melody Ermachild Chavis
ALTARS IN THE STREET
A Courageous Memoir of Community and Spiritual Awakening
A deeply moving account that captures
the essence of human struggles and resourcefulness.
0-609-80196-1 Softcover

Tracy Cochran and Jeff Zaleski
TRANSFORMATIONS
Awakening to the Sacred in Ourselves
An exploration of enlightenment experiences and
the ways in which they can transform our lives.
0-517-70150-2 Hardcover

David A. Cooper
ENTERING THE SACRED MOUNTAIN
Exploring the Mystical Practices of Judaism, Buddhism, and Sufism
An inspiring chronicle of one man's search for truth.
0-517-88464-X Softcover

Marc David
NOURISHING WISDOM
A Mind/Body Approach to Nutrition and Well-Being
A book that advocates awareness in eating.
0-517-88129-2 Softcover

Kat Duff
THE ALCHEMY OF ILLNESS
A luminous inquiry into the function and purpose of illness.
0-517-88097-0 Softcover

Joan Furman, MSN, RN, and David McNabb
THE DYING TIME
Practical Wisdom for the Dying and Their Caregivers
A comprehensive guide, filled with physical, emotional, and spiritual advice.
0-609-80003-5 Softcover

Bernard Glassman
BEARING WITNESS
A Zen Master's Lessons in Making Peace
How Glassman started the Zen Peacemaker Order and
what each of us can do to make peace in our hearts and in the world.
0-609-80391-3 Softcover

Bernard Glassman and Rick Fields
INSTRUCTIONS TO THE COOK
A Zen Master's Lessons in Living a Life that Matters
A distillation of Zen wisdom that can be used equally well as
a manual on business or spiritual practice, cooking or life.
0-517-88829-7 Softcover

Burghild Nina Holzer
A WALK BETWEEN HEAVEN AND EARTH
A Personal Journal on Writing and the Creative Process
How keeping a journal focuses and expands our awareness
of ourselves and everything that touches our lives.
0-517-88096-2 Softcover

Greg Johanson and Ron Kurtz
GRACE UNFOLDING
Psychotherapy in the Spirit of the Tao-te ching
The interaction of client and therapist illuminated
through the gentle power and wisdom of Lao Tsu's ancient classic.
0-517-88130-6 Softcover

Jack and Marcia Kelly
SANCTUARIES
A Guide to Lodgings in Monasteries, Abbeys, and Retreats
of the United States
For those in search of renewal and a little peace;
described by the *New York Times* as "the *Michelin Guide* of the retreat set."
0-517-88517-4 Softcover

Selected by Marcia and Jack Kelly
ONE HUNDRED GRACES
Mealtime Blessings
A collection of graces from many traditions,
inscribed in calligraphy reminiscent of the manuscripts of medieval Europe.
0-517-58567-7 Hardcover
0-609-80093-0 Softcover

Marcia and Jack Kelly
THE WHOLE HEAVEN CATALOG
A Resource Guide to Products, Services, Arts, Crafts, and Festivals
of Religious, Spiritual, and Cooperative Communities
All the things that monks and nuns do to support their habits!
0-609-80120-1 Softcover

Barbara Lachman
THE JOURNAL OF HILDEGARD OF BINGEN
A year in the life of the twelfth-century German saint—
the diary she never had the time to write herself.
0-517-88390-2 Softcover

Stephen Levine
A YEAR TO LIVE
How to Live This Year as if It Were Your Last
Using the consciousness of our mortality
to enter into a new and vibrant relationship with life.
0-609-80194-5 Softcover

Gunilla Norris
BEING HOME
A Book of Meditations
An exquisite modern book of hours,
a celebration of mindfulness in everyday activities.
0-517-58159-0 Hardcover

Marcia Prager
THE PATH OF BLESSING
Experiencing the Energy and Abundance of the Divine
How to use the traditional Jewish practice of calling down a blessing
on each action as a profound path of spiritual growth.
0-517-70363-7 Hardcover
0-609-80393-X Softcover

Ram Dass and Mirabai Bush
COMPASSION IN ACTION
Setting Out on the Path of Service
Heartfelt encouragement and advice for those ready
to commit time and energy to relieving suffering in the world.
0-517-88500-X Softcover

Saki Santorelli
HEAL THY SELF
Lessons on Mindfulness in Medicine
An invitation to patients and health care professionals to bring mindfulness
into the crucible of the healing relationship.
0-609-60385-X Hardcover

Rabbi Rami M. Shapiro
MINYAN
Ten Principles for Living a Life of Integrity
A primer for those interested to know
what Judaism has to offer the spiritually hungry.
0-609-80055-8 Softcover

Rabbi Rami M. Shapiro
WISDOM OF THE JEWISH SAGES
A Modern Reading of Pirke Avot
A third-century treasury of maxims on justice, integrity, and virtue—
Judaism's principal ethical scripture.
0-517-79966-9 Hardcover

James Thornton
A FIELD GUIDE TO THE SOUL
A Down-to-Earth Handbook of Spiritual Practice
A manual for coming into harmony and communion with the earth.
0-609-60368-X Hardcover

Joan Tollifson
BARE-BONES MEDITATION
Waking Up from the Story of My Life
An unvarnished, exhilarating account of one woman's struggle
to make sense of her life.
0-517-88792-4 Softcover

Michael Toms and Justine Willis Toms
TRUE WORK
Doing What You Love and Loving What You Do
Wisdom for the workplace from the husband-and-wife team
of NPR's weekly radio program *New Dimensions.*
0-609-80212-7 Softcover

BUDDHA LAUGHING
A Tricycle *Book of Cartoons*
A marvelous opportunity for self-reflection
for those who tend to take themselves too seriously.
0-609-80409-X Softcover

Ed. Richard Whelan
SELF-RELIANCE
The Wisdom of Ralph Waldo Emerson as Inspiration for Daily Living
A distillation of Emerson's spiritual writings for contemporary readers.
0-517-58512-X Softcover

Bell Tower books are for sale at your local bookstore
or you may call Random House at 1-800-793-BOOK to order with a credit card.